Disunity

in Christ

*Uncovering the Hidden
Forces That Keep Us Apart*

CHRISTENA CLEVELAND

IVP Books

An imprint of InterVarsity Press
Downers Grove, Illinois

InterVarsity Press
P.O. Box 1400, Downers Grove, IL 60515-1426
World Wide Web: www.ivpress.com
Email: email@ivpress.com

InterVarsity Press® is the book-publishing division of InterVarsity Christian Fellowship/USA®, a movement of students and faculty active on campus at hundreds of universities, colleges and schools of nursing in the United States of America, and a member movement of the International Fellowship of Evangelical Students. For information about local and regional activities, write Public Relations Dept., InterVarsity Christian Fellowship/USA, 6400 Schroeder Rd., P.O. Box 7895, Madison, WI 53707-7895, or visit the IVCF website at www.intervarsity.org.

All Scripture quotations, unless otherwise indicated, are taken from THE HOLY BIBLE, NEW INTERNATIONAL VERSION®, NIV® Copyright © 1973, 1978, 1984, 2011 by Biblica, Inc.™ Used by permission. All rights reserved worldwide.

While all stories in this book are true, some names and identifying information in this book have been changed to protect the privacy of the individuals involved.

Design: David Fassett
Interior design: Beth Hagenberg
Images: wooden chair: ©vm/iStockphoto
   primed canvas: ©Chris Schmidt/iStockphoto

ISBN 978-0-8308-4403-6 (print)
ISBN 978-0-8308-6495-9 (digital)

Printed in the United States of America ∞

Library of Congress Cataloging-in-Publication Data

Cleveland, Christena, 1980-
 Disunity in Christ : uncovering the hidden forces that keep us apart /
Christena Cleveland.
 pages cm
Includes bibliographical references.
ISBN 978-0-8308-4403-6 (pbk. : alk. paper)
1. Church—Unity. 2. Church controversies. I. Title.
BV601.5.C54 2013
262'.72—dc23

                      2013024551

P	17	16	15	14	13	12	11	10	9	8	7	6
Y	27	26	25	24	23	22	21	20	19	18	17	16

For my sister, Des

Contents

Acknowledgments

It's a good thing I love adventures because writing this book has been quite the adventure. Thankfully, I have had some stellar individuals by my side as I've worked on the most fun and challenging writing project I've ever done.

First, I'd like to thank my editor, Andy Le Peau, and the folks at InterVarsity Press for patient guidance as I navigated the highs and lows of writing my first book. I'd also like to thank the two anonymous reviewers who provided helpful feedback on an early draft.

I'm grateful for my Southern California pastors Billy and Kristin Calderwood and my Minneapolis pastors Jeff and Le Que Heidkamp. I'm at my best when I'm working on a team with other people who are much wiser and cooler than I am. Thanks for being my cooler, wiser teammates! I'm especially appreciative of Billy, who taught me the power of hope and helped me cultivate my voice, strength and calling to lead others into unity.

I'm indebted to my social psychology mentors, Jay Hull at Dartmouth and Jim Blascovich and Stan Klein at UC Santa Barbara, who have spent years helping me to think critically and acquire strong research skills. I'm particularly grateful to Jay, who lured me away from the religious studies department, offered me a position in his social cognition lab and convinced me to get undergraduate and graduate degrees in psychology. It was the right move for me, and it set me on the path to write this book.

Many thanks to Curtiss DeYoung for befriending me as soon as I arrived in the Twin Cities, mentoring me in the words and deeds of reconciliation and modeling how to empower diverse others.

I'm thankful for my forever friends Mardi, Emily, Ronee and Patrick, who I can always trust to have my back, as well as my prayer partners Elle, Stacy and Cristin, who provided lovingly strict accountability as I finished this book. I'm also grateful for my friends who pray for me when I'm writing and speaking: Rose, Maura, Tim, Avivah, Jon, Michelle, Julie, Jina, Juanita, Erica, Josie, Elisa and Ricardo. I feel clothed in their prayers even though many are far away.

I'm so glad to be part of a family that is committed to loving well across cultural differences. My dad is the best intercultural leader I know. I was fortunate to inherit not only his crosscultural DNA but also his passion for ministry. My mom's commitment to lifelong spiritual growth inspires me to maintain a teachable and humble posture. My super smart brother, John, knows how to disagree agreeably and models how to love well while effectively schooling people. And my sister, Des, is the best listener and most caring person I know. I learn from all of them, and in countless ways they have contributed to this book.

Last, I give honor to Jesus Christ, the author of unity and the chief reconciler.

1

Right Christian,
Wrong Christian

I was taking a bus ride through the snow-capped Rockies in Colorado, complaining to myself about this guy at my church who drove me crazy. Ben and I were pretty much the only unmarried adults in our small church community, so we were often paired together during social events. As if this weren't annoying enough, Ben happened to be quite possibly the most offensive person I knew.

I wish I could say this wasn't the case, but everything about Ben bugged me—from his inflexible and preachy conservatism to his career as an engineer who designs nuclear warheads (I mean, *seriously?*) to his dorky Hawaiian-print button-downs (alas, perhaps his greatest offense). Anyway, there I was riding through Colorado, lamenting the fact that Ben was a part of my life and plotting ways to avoid interacting with him ever again. And suddenly I was confronted with the idea that Ben was going to be in heaven.

With me.

For all eternity.

And I would never, ever be rid of him.

Suddenly the idea of frolicking on the streets of gold seemed less enticing. *That's okay*, I quickly reassured myself. *Heaven is going to be a big, big place.*

Growing the Wrong Way

When I first began walking with Christ, I felt an immediate and authentic connection with any other Christian who crossed my path. Orthodox, Catholic, charismatic, Lutheran, evangelical, black, white, Asian, Ben—didn't matter. We were family.

But as I walked with Jesus, somehow my "growth" had been coupled with increasingly stronger opinions about the "right" way to be a follower. I started keeping people I didn't enjoy or agree with at arm's length. I managed to avoid most of the Bens in my life by locating them, categorizing them and gracefully shunning them, all while appearing to be both spiritual and community-oriented. Further, I could do all of this without wasting any of my precious brainpower. I was quite good.

I chose to build community with people with whom I could pretty much agree on everything. I invested lots of time and energy in fostering relationships with people who had similar ethnic backgrounds, were about my age, possessed similar educational degrees, professed similar theology, worshiped like me, voted like me and were fluent in the language of my postmodern, intellectual, wanderlustful, "diverse" culture. I sincerely thought that I was doing a fabulous job because, hey, I was "living in community," and isn't that what good Christians are supposed to do?

Over time, when I met other Christians, I found myself asking them what church they attended. Some answers were more acceptable than others. The way I saw it, there were two types of Christians: the wrong kind of Christian and the right kind of Christian.

It was that simple.

Wrong Christian was not a thinker. He hadn't read a book in the previous two years and had the limited vocabulary to prove it. (Although, come to think of it, he did read a book a few years back about a woman's rightful place in the home.) He voted based on one or two issues: abortion and homosexuality (two issues that Jesus didn't even mention *once*, mind you). Wrong Christian lacked crosscultural sensitivity and somehow managed to avoid spending quality time with anyone who did not share his race and culture.

Naturally, he only dated women within his race, although he occasionally crushed on more "exotic" types. When he was not rockin' the suburbs in his gas-guzzling SUV, he surfed or played ultimate or some other inane "sport." He proudly served in the United States military and inexplicably (to me) was more concerned with the preservation of the Second Amendment than the First. He was a card-carrying and proselytizing Calvinist. In fact, the last time I was over at his house, I noticed that the acronym TULIP was boldly painted above his door. He voted Republican! Republican! Republican!

And he was a *he*. Seriously, did you expect Wrong Christian to be a woman? Pshaw.

Curiously, Right Christian was a lot more like me. While driving her Prius en route to the farmer's market, she self-righteously zipped past Wrong Christian's lumbering SUV, blithely unaware of the fact that Prius owners (and farmer's market shoppers, who are basically the same people) are consumers, just like everyone else.

She was a woman of the world; she was well traveled and able to thrive in any cultural setting (except for those conservative Christian ones in the flyover states, naturally). She boasted of the ethnic diversity of her friend group and joked that she and her friends looked like they had just walked off the pages of a United Colors of Benetton clothing ad. (Despite her high IQ—or perhaps due to it—she overlooked the fact that as well-educated, upwardly mobile, frequent Benetton shoppers, she and her friends were perhaps not as diverse as they thought.) She hopped onto the poverty, social justice and environmental bandwagons as well as any other bandwagons that were in vogue at the time.

She wasn't bound by political party affiliation. Rather, she thought for herself and voted independently (in other words, she voted Democrat! Democrat! Democrat!). Right Christian was a reader and a writer. In fact, she'd *written* more books than Wrong Christian had read. She was an equal-opportunity dater. (Translation: she'd date anybody but Wrong Christian and his buddies.) She was strong. She knew that she was wonderful, charming and, quite frankly, a more valuable member of the body of Christ than Wrong Christian. All of these characteristics (and many, *many* more) made her Right Christian.

So it all began with two labels: Right Christian and Wrong Christian. The funny thing is, the more I talk with people about these labels, the more I realize that many of us carry our own descriptions of Right Christian and Wrong Christian. Perhaps in your opinion, my Right Christian is your Wrong Christian and my Wrong Christian is your Right Christian. Or maybe your Wrong Christian and Right Christian are totally different birds.

Recently, a friend told me that he's not willing to attend a particular church in our town because the last time he visited this church, he noticed a young man wearing a baseball cap during the worship service. According to my friend, Wrong Christian is an irreverent little twerp who wears baseball caps during church. Maybe this isn't your issue. I have another dear friend who is unable to talk about charismatic churches without a noticeable amount of disdain in his tone of voice. To him, Wrong Christian is a charismatic guy who speaks in tongues and worships weirdly.

Maybe to you, Wrong Christian attends a church that allows female leadership. Or maybe Wrong Christian attends a church that *doesn't* allow female leadership. Maybe Wrong Christian went to a Christian college. Maybe Wrong Christian doesn't speak English. Maybe Wrong Christian is in a college fraternity. Maybe Wrong Christian drives a Hummer. Maybe Wrong Christian promotes Reformed theology. Maybe Wrong Christian dresses like she's in a music video. Maybe Wrong Christian is pro-choice. Maybe Wrong Christian takes the bus. Maybe Wrong Christian is just annoying. Maybe Wrong Christian is unequivocally pro-Israel. Maybe Wrong Christian is a Yankees fan.

You get the picture.

My opinion of Wrong Christian was so strong that I not only avoided him, but I also actively condemned him. Perhaps you're not as opinionated as I am (although I'm sure many of you are). Maybe you have opinions but don't voice them in a forceful and condescending way. Or maybe you don't voice them at all—you're not around Wrong Christian very much, so you're not devoting a lot of time and energy to criticizing him. He's so far outside your circle of (Right) Christians that he barely exists. The mere act of creating Right Christian and Wrong Christian labels makes Wrong Christians a target of your criticism or simply dead to you—or both.

For the most part, I was happy to keep Wrong Christian at bay. There was just one cosmic problem. As I got to know Jesus, I began to realize that this was not exactly what he had in mind when he invited us to participate in his kingdom on earth.

I discovered that Jesus apparently didn't get the memo concerning the colossal importance of my distinction between Right Christian and Wrong Christian. In fact, he doesn't seem to care much for this distinction at all. I think this is what God meant when he said, "So are my ways higher than your ways and my thoughts than your thoughts" in Isaiah 55:9.

There I was, convinced that I was defending Jesus by condemning Wrong Christian, when I saw that Jesus was beckoning both Right Christian *and* Wrong Christian and inviting all of us to know more of his heart. As I read through the Gospels, I noticed that he had a habit of connecting with everybody: conservative theologians, liberal theologians, prostitutes, divorcees, children, politicians, people who party hard, military servicemen, women, lepers, ethnic minorities, celebrities, you name it. He was pretty serious about connecting, in spite of natural and ideological differences. And it doesn't end in the Gospels. He repeatedly disregards my Right Christian and Wrong Christian labels and continues to beckon me, even though I still tend to cling to such earthly distinctions. He's relentless.

Rather than using his power to distance himself from us, Jesus uses it to approach us. He follows his own commandment to love your neighbor as yourself—often to his detriment, I might add— by pursuing *us* with great tenacity in spite of our differences. He jumps a lot of hurdles to reach us.

Jesus, Unity and Fenway Park

About halfway through my graduate school program, I decided that I wanted a career in Major League Baseball. As a lifelong baseball fan—it's such a cerebral sport—and a budding social psychologist who studied group motivation, this wasn't an entirely ridiculous idea. At any rate, a few months later, I said goodbye to my research lab in California and moved to Boston to intern with the Boston Red Sox organization for a summer.

During those marvelous months, I became close friends with another intern named Sam. During our lunch breaks, we often sat in the empty grandstands at Fenway Park and talked about life, faith, good books and friends. Even though we often specifically talked about my relationship with Jesus, the summer was halfway over before Sam realized that I was an actual Christian. And let me tell you, he was not a fan of this idea.

He punched the seat in front of him.

"You're not a Christian," he insisted, vigorously shaking his head for extra effect.

"How's that?" I asked. I was confused.

"You're not like other Christians, Christena," he told me. "You're not judgmental and ignorant and dogmatic and anti-intellectual. Don't call yourself a Christian."

Sam was fired up.

"Well, I'm a follower of Christ, so by definition I'm a Christian." It was that simple to me.

"But you shouldn't associate with all of those ridiculous people who call themselves Christians. It makes you look bad," Sam responded.

I thought it was sweet of him to care about my reputation. I also thought it was sweet of him to think that I *wasn't* judgmental and ignorant and dogmatic and anti-intellectual.

This is when it occurred to me that Sam hadn't been introduced to the beauty and strength of Jesus' heart. Sam, like many other people, had no idea that Jesus pursues us in spite of the fact that we are all judgmental, ignorant, dogmatic and anti-intellectual at times. It also occurred to me that perhaps these sorts of conversations are why Jesus invites us to imitate him in pursuing each other. We represent Jesus well when we draw near to other believers, regardless of differences. This is how we show unbelievers Jesus' heart. And this is how we invite them to join us in following him. We need to be reminded of Jesus' words: "By this everyone will know that you are my disciples, if you love one another" (John 13:35).

And so I looked Sam in the eye and grinned. "Jesus doesn't distance himself from me even though, let's face it, I'm not always good for PR. I can do the same for other Christians."

He was shocked and suspicious. The idea was intriguing, but not at all logical. In Sam's world, you don't pal around with people who could ruin your reputation. But that sunny Boston day, right in the middle of the aging grandstands at Fenway Park, he saw a tiny bit of Jesus' heart. It's not logical, but it's definitely relational.

By walking in friendship with Sam (and many others like him), I have learned that the more we follow Christ's example by relinquishing Right Christian/Wrong Christian labels and crossing the boundaries of our world, the better we represent his vision to the world. This is both beautiful and scary to me. The beautiful part is easy to talk about. I desperately want my friends to experience Jesus' heart. I bet you feel as strongly as I do.

I'm Not Making *These* Points

Before we continue our (admittedly one-sided) conversation, I'd like to be clear about what I am *not* saying. One, I'm not saying that differences in the body of Christ are trivial. I'm not suggesting that we just forget about our substantive, ideological differences or that we refrain from making strong statements concerning how we view faith in God and how we live out our faith in practical ways so we can happily move on to singing "Kumbaya" and making s'mores.

There's an analogy that wise King Solomon used to describe a good friendship. He said that two friends sharpen each other like iron sharpens iron (see Proverbs 27:17). I think it's curious that he chose iron, a material that is known for its strength and solidity, to describe a good friend. According to Solomon, a good friendship isn't a moral free-for-all, in which any difference is accepted or glossed over. Rather, a good friendship involves a healthy tension in which the friends challenge and encourage each other to draw closer to the heart of God. Each friend uses her strength to help the other friend grow stronger. Friends who share their different ideas about faith or life can help us to avoid some of the nasty effects of group polarization that I'll talk about later. Essentially, they draw us out of our own world and in doing so, help us to stay away from Right Christian/Wrong Christian labels.

Besides, principles and theology are important. They certainly fueled a lot of what Jesus did for us on the cross. Yes, we do need to have candid conversations about racial injustice in the church and beyond, how we're interacting with the natural environment, how we're caring for the homeless, how we're protecting the unborn, how we're defining atonement, who we are voting for and so forth. These are all necessary and valuable conversations.

The trick is to wisely use our Christian friends' ideology to humble us, strengthen us and enhance our understanding of God and the role we're called to play in his kingdom. And we should influence our friends in the same way. Like iron sharpens iron. This is a huge and complicated idea that warrants much more discussion. I'm looking forward to returning to this idea later on in our conversation.

Two, I am not saying that cultural differences within the body of Christ are inconsequential or petty. There's a "surfer" church in Santa Barbara, where I used to live. The church is located a couple of blocks from the beach, and the pastor is pretty well known in the global surf community. If you visit this church, you'll see lots of surfers and skaters and other types who typically associate with surfers and skaters. In his sermons, the pastor often uses examples from surfing to explain his points. I know very little about surfing (or why people would voluntarily get up at 4 a.m. to go jump in the freezing cold ocean), so his surf illustrations usually just leave me confused. But I notice that all of the surfers and skaters seem to nod appreciatively whenever he uses these examples. So in that sense, I'm all for the surfing analogies, and by extension, the surfer church.

Three, I am not saying that this crazy idea of dropping our labels in search of unity is easy. There are some real hurdles that make it difficult for different individuals and different groups to come together in healthy, meaningful and lasting ways. Hopefully our conversation in this book will help to demystify some of these hurdles and give you both the understanding and the hope to say goodbye to divisions in the body of Christ.

Ben, Again

Remember Ben, the poor guy I blasted at the beginning of the chapter? A few summers back, Santa Barbara was subjected to a series of devastating wildfires. We're talking fires of biblical pro-

portions; the whole city was covered in smoke and soot for most of
the month of July. One of the wildfires threatened the homes of
several people in our church community.

Most of us were backing away from the area affected by the fires,
tending to our power outages, shutting our windows and so forth. But
Ben was approaching the fire zone, checking on people in the church,
offering to do anything to help them. He did this in spite of the fact
that many of the people to whom he was offering help hailed from
different ethnic backgrounds, voted for different candidates, held opposing eschatological views and dressed differently.

During that summer, Ben showed me what it looks like to relativize differences in order to love each other in sacrificial ways. As
a member of the family of God, Ben uniquely demonstrates the
character of Jesus. Ben is essential to me, and I would never have
recognized this if I had forever cast him as Wrong Christian.

This revelation about Ben makes me wonder if our understanding of Jesus (and by extension, our role as his followers) is
limited by our inability to see him represented in the diversity of
the body of Christ. I wonder how much Christ's heart is broken
when we denigrate followers of Christ who differ from us. I shudder
at the thought of it.

Further, how much are we losing because of our differences?
How much are the people for whom Christ died suffering because
we remain paralyzed and divided by our differences when we
should be working together as the hands and feet of Jesus in the
world? There must be a better and more efficient way to carry out
our roles within the mission of God. Surely, we can do better.

Cultural differences in the body of Christ enable different types
of people to draw near to the heart of Jesus. As his church, I'm
grateful that we can follow in his example of being all things to all
people. Jesus did a fantastic job of knowing his audience and
speaking directly to their hearts. For example, Jesus talked sheep
to shepherds, fish to fishermen, and bookish theology to bookish

theologians. He was all things to all people. I think that our differences enable us to speak richly and directly to the hearts of all types of people.

As we'll discover in the following chapter, culturally homogenous churches are adept at targeting and attracting a certain type of person and creating a strong group identity. However, attendees at such churches are at a higher risk for creating the overly simplistic and divisive Right Christian and Wrong Christian labels that dangerously lead to inaccurate perceptions of other Christians as well as hostility and conflict. What often begins as an effective and culturally specific way to reach people for Christ ends up stifling their growth as disciples. Perhaps this is because we often fail to make a distinction between evangelism and discipleship. People can *meet* God within their cultural context but in order to *follow* God, they must cross into other cultures because that's what Jesus did in the incarnation and on the cross. Discipleship is crosscultural. When we meet Jesus around people who are just like us and then continue to follow Jesus with people who are just like us, we stifle our growth in Christ and open ourselves up to a world of division. However, when we're rubbing elbows in Christian fellowship with people who are different from us, we can learn from each other and grow more like Christ. Like iron sharpens iron.

For this reason, I believe that churches and Christian organizations should strive for cultural diversity. Regardless of ethnic demographics, every community is multicultural when one considers the various cultures of age, gender, economic status, education level, political orientation and so on. Further, every church should fully utilize the multifaceted cultural diversity within itself, express the diversity of its local community, expertly welcome the other, embrace all who are members of the body of Christ and intentionally collaborate with different churches or organizations in order to impact the kingdom. And churches situated in multiethnic communities—I'm not letting you off the hook—should absolutely be ethnically diverse.

Overcoming differences. Working through conflict. Seeing culturally different others as God's gift to us rather than thorns in the flesh. That's what this book is about. The causes of these problems can be devilishly subtle. Sometimes they don't simply reside in our individual personalities, defects and sins. Sometimes we are affected in hidden ways by those around us. The values and perceptions of the groups with which we identify can have a covert effect on us. Unpacking those dynamics and how we can turn them to God's glory is also what this book is about.

In the following chapters, I will use insights from social psychology to help us understand the unseen dynamics of how church-related homogenous groups form, why they persist, how they affect our behavior, thoughts and emotions, and how they create seemingly insurmountable hurdles that divide the body of Christ. We'll also discuss the many ways in which we can overcome these hurdles. (It turns out that they're absolutely surmountable.) And we'll get a glimpse of just how much the body of Christ can impact the world in incredible ways.

Chapter 1 Questions

1. Do you have labels for Right Christian and Wrong Christian? If yes, how would you describe them?

2. We often create labels for Right Christian and Wrong Christian without consciously thinking about it. Where do these labels come from? How do we decide who is Right Christian and who is Wrong Christian?

3. Do you think God can use Wrong Christian to sharpen you? If yes, how so? If no, why not?

4. How do you think unbelievers perceive disunity between Christians? How do you think disunity between Christians affects unbelievers?

5. Do you think churches and Christian organizations should be multicultural? Why/why not?

6. Think about the ethnic and cultural demographics in your community. Does your church reflect those demographics? If not, why not?

2

How Divisions Are Killing Us
and Why We Should Care

I suspect I am not alone in having drawn comfort from believing that heaven is going to be really, really big, and that I wouldn't have to bump into annoying people too much, the way I thought of my friend Ben. Sure, I looked forward to meeting the best version of myself and exploring a fully renewed physical world. Plus, the thought of seeing Jesus face-to-face sparked light in even the darkest corners of my heart. All of these things—Perfect Me, the renewed physical world, Jesus—sounded fabulous. The problem was the other people who are going to be there.

At the time I reassured myself that heaven was probably going to be a lot like Chicago. If you've ever spent time in Chicago, you may have noticed that the city is beautiful and diverse but also astoundingly segregated. In fact, Chicago was recently named the most segregated city in America. Maybe heaven would be too!

Due to Chicago's twenty-three distinct, linguistically isolated ethnic neighborhoods, people can easily surround themselves with similar others and avoid interactions with other ethnic groups. When it comes to predicting behavior, this neighborhood pattern is actually quite useful.

By simply knowing a person's race, you can predict where they live and even what teams they will root for. In Chicago many black people live on the South side and lots of white people live on the North side. Blacks tend to be White Sox fans, and whites tend to be Cubs fans.

Personality psychologist Kevin Stolarick has found that by simply knowing a Chicago resident's personality, you can predict where they live. According to Kathy Bergen in an article on Stolarick's findings, "People who view themselves as extroverted and agreeable tend to cluster on the South Side, while more experimental types with neurotic tendencies are living to the north and along the lake."

To be fair, cultural isolation is natural and comforting; we tend to cling to like-minded group members and keep others at bay. However, the Windy City's historically segregated landscape discourages mutually beneficial crosscultural interactions and is a known breeding ground for crosscultural conflict and misunderstanding.

On the bright side, the segregation sure cuts down on messy and historically charged interactions with those who are different. And like the good citizens of Chicago, those messy interactions were just the things that I was hoping to avoid both on earth and later on in heaven. So heaven will be like Chicago, I told myself. I'm sure we'll all gravitate toward our own kind.

There will be a German neighborhood and a Catholic neighborhood and a Korean neighborhood and a liberal neighborhood that borders an environmentally friendly neighborhood and a Methodist neighborhood that maintains a garden co-op with the Independent Freewill neighborhood and an emerging-church neighborhood that frequents the same pub as the Episcopal neighborhood. And I'll spend all of my time worshiping Jesus within the neighborhood of my choice, occasionally interacting with people from other acceptable neighborhoods. And no annoying Christians will ever disrupt my peaceful eternity in Chicago heaven.

Evangelical Consumerism

Unfortunately, Chicago seems to be a blueprint for Christians when thinking about the kingdom of God. In theory, we support the vision of a diverse, integrated and interdependent body of Christ, but we certainly don't want to venture outside of our neighborhoods to live the vision.

We have Reformed churches, black churches, hipster churches, Chinese churches, Pentecostal churches, emerging churches—but we rarely engage in meaningful interactions outside of our church groups. Instead, we tend to focus on the things that differentiate us from other groups, underestimate the richness and value that other groups bring to the kingdom of God and foster negative attitudes about other groups. If we interact with other groups at all, we usually do so at a distance and with at least a hint of suspicion. If we are a body, then we are one that is afflicted with an autoimmune disease.

Political scientists Naomi Cahn and June Carbone have noted that in the 1960s, geographic boundaries rather than culture and ideology largely determined church membership. So the typical American churchgoer attended a neighborhood church. Consequently, the diversity of the church congregation reflected the diversity of the neighborhood. To the extent that the neighborhood was ethnically, politically and socioeconomically diverse, the church was too.

Today's churchgoers, by contrast, tend to shop for churches that express their individual values and are culturally similar. We often drive by dozens of churches en route to our church, the one that meets our cultural expectations. American society has engaged in an evangelical spiritual consumerism that some scholars pejoratively call "Burger King Christianity." As a result, individuals who, albeit unconsciously, manage to exit adolescence without interacting across cultural lines can easily evolve into churchgoers who continue to maintain these divisions in culturally homogenous churches. Ultimately, homogeneity within churches lives on while meaningful crosscultural and cross-ideological interactions are limited.

These days, Christians can easily go their entire lives without spending time with those who are different from them. Unfortunately, the more we spend time with people who are essentially identical to us, the more we become convinced that our way of relating to both Jesus and the world is *the* correct way. Over time, our convictions grow stronger and our attitudes toward different ideas and cultural expressions of worship become more negative.

Social psychologists call this phenomenon *group polarization*. In the absence of diverse influences, homogenous group members tend to adopt more extreme and narrow-minded thinking as time passes. In chapter 4, I'll talk about how and why this occurs. For now, suffice it to say that it simply happens. It certainly happened to me. That's why I found myself wondering whether I'd want to spend eternity with a bunch of people who didn't act and think just like me.

Many pastors have also felt the distressing effects of divisions in the body of Christ. One white pastor who had recently experienced a disappointing crosscultural ministry partnership with a nearby black pastor recounted his frustration, saying to me with fear and pain in his eyes, "Black pastors like [the pastor with whom he had been working] make white pastors like me want to give up on unity." With compassion, I assured him that many black pastors have said the same thing about white pastors. When it comes to uniting across cultural divides, even the best intentions often yield discouraging results. But no one seems to know why divisions are so persistent.

Sometimes it seems as though invisible forces are thwarting church leaders' best-intentioned efforts to build unity. If we can uncover the dynamics that divide us (whether ethnic, political, theological or cultural), we can begin to devise a plan for beating them. Insights from social psychology on group processes can help us to understand *why* such divisions exist and *how* we can overcome them in healthy, fruitful ways. Such research can help us understand why we often draw strong lines between *us* and *them*, why our lines often evolve into value judgments (that is, *we* are right and *they* are wrong) and why our perceptions of *them* are often inaccurate and negative.

The Power of the Familiar

As Cahn and Carbone have noted, American churches are increasing in ethnic, cultural and theological homogeneity despite the fact that America is becoming increasingly diverse. Indeed, sociologists Michael Emerson and Christian Smith point out that over 90 percent of all American churches are composed of congregations that are at least 90 percent racially homogenous. Further, theologian Scot McKnight suggests that the same processes that contribute to a lack of ethnic/racial diversity in churches are also contributing to ideological and theological homogeneity. Not only do we look the same, we also think the same. Martin Luther King's famous assessment that "At 11 a.m. Sunday morning . . . we stand at the most segregated hour in this nation" is, sadly, as true as ever.

For both emotional and cognitive reasons, the process of forming and maintaining groups with people who are similar to us is logical, natural and powerful. From an emotional point of view, it makes sense that we prefer to spend time with and worship with people who are familiar to us and similar to us.

Research on interpersonal attraction suggests that familiarity is *the* most powerful predictor of friendship. The more we interact with a person, the more familiar we become with them. The more familiar we become with them, the more we like them. Sir Peter Ustinov writes, "Contrary to popular belief, I do not believe that friends are necessarily the people you like best, they are merely the people who got there first."

For survival reasons, this makes a lot of sense. If an individual seems vaguely familiar to me because I have seen her around my neighborhood a few times, I can quickly assume that she is safe because, as far as I know, she hasn't tried to harm me. If I perceive her as safe, I'll automatically like her more than someone who is completely unfamiliar and thus possibly unsafe. If a woman is unfamiliar to me, I do not have any information on whether she is trustworthy or not, so I am less likely to assume trustworthiness. Ultimately, I'm more drawn to the woman who is familiar and am more likely to start a friendship with her. The old wives' tale is wrong: familiarity breeds liking, not contempt.

One research study revealed that people rate individuals they hazily recall seeing somewhere but don't fully recognize as more honest, intelligent and physically attractive than individuals who are completely unfamiliar. People also express more interest in hanging out with and working on collaborative projects with somewhat familiar individuals compared to unfamiliar individuals. Apparently, we like people who are somewhat familiar to us even if we can't specifically recall seeing them before!

Here's the conundrum for the church: If people who *seem* familiar are perceived as more likable and people who are completely unfamiliar are perceived as less likable, we're going to naturally befriend the people who *seem* familiar. And the people who *seem* familiar are the ones that we see around us—our neighbors, fellow students at our schools and people in our church. Unfortunately, many Christians live among, study with and worship with people who are pretty much just like them. Consequently, the people who are simply around us happen to be a lot like us, and the people who are different from us are beyond our radar.

It's no wonder that we are drawn to people who are just like us—they're the only ones around us! Our homogeneity is like a cage surrounding our group, preventing us from becoming familiar with culturally different others.

What Binds Us Together

Confession: I love it when the people around me agree with my opinions and values and applaud me for simply being me. Research suggests that we all love this. In addition to liking familiar others, we like similar others because they affirm our worldviews, behaviors and experiences. We especially like people who hail from similar demographic groups (age, education, race, religion, socioeconomic status, etc.), possess similar attitudes and have endured similar experiences.

One classic researcher named Theodore Newcomb created an experimental college dormitory and filled it with students who agreed to live in the dorm and participate in the study. Newcomb found that students who were racially and/or religiously similar grew to like each other more than those who were dissimilar. More recent research suggests that this preference for those who are demographically similar remains strong.

Quite simply, we like people who are like us; we are attracted to people who share the same attitudes, values and preferences. Similarity is one of the most important predictors of liking because we like people who can affirm our worldviews and share our experiences. As an unmarried, urban, professional woman of color, I simply like other women who share these characteristics. My interactions with them are easier because we speak the same "language," roll our eyes at the same things and can easily rejoice and commiserate with each other. Dissimilar people don't "get" my humor or laugh at my jokes. This is a problem because I like to think of myself as funny.

Research shows that sharing an experience with another person—sometimes called "I-sharing"—causes people to feel a profound sense of connection with others, even others who are otherwise dissimilar. Even brief, seemingly inconsequential experiences can help you to connect with others. Imagine you hear a stranger ahead of you in the grocery checkout line say something that strikes you as funny. You glance at the person in line behind you, who glances back, and the two of you burst out laughing, as if you share a private joke. This shared experience increases your liking for this stranger, even if you and the stranger have almost nothing in common.

This idea of shared experiences can help us understand why Christians often form strong bonds with people who share their *very* specific experiences and keep even slightly different others at bay. Christians are so good at erecting divisions that we don't stop at the major ones (e.g., race/ethnicity, class and gender); we also create divisions *within* divisions. For example, while the body of Christ experiences significant intergender (man vs. woman) division, it is also plagued by *intra*gender (woman vs. woman and man vs. man) division. For example, Christian women contribute to divisions between egalitarians and complementarians, stay-at-home moms and working moms (the infamous "Mommy Wars"), feminists and traditionalists, married women who take their husband's last name and married women who don't, unmarried and married women, urban and suburban women, black and white women, mothers and nonmothers, and young and old women, to name just a few. The women in these specific groups are profoundly bound by their shared experiences. As a result, they tend to gravitate toward those who share their experiences and away from those who do not.

Pinel and her colleagues believe that shared experiences can be a powerful unifier, rather than a divider. They explain, "A fundamentalist Christian and an atheist can find themselves enjoying the same sunset; a staunch Republican and an equally staunch Democrat can share a laugh. When two objectively different people I-share in these and other ways, their disliking for one another might lessen, if only for a moment." However, since we spend most of our time with people who are demographically and attitudinally similar to us, our most common shared experi-

ences are with people who look, think, act and experience the
world like us, which further solidifies our bond with them and
increases our liking for them. As a result, we fall deeper into our
homogeneity.

The Snowball Effect

Comedian Emo Phillips wrote a joke about divisions among Christians. Apparently, the joke is hilarious; *GQ* magazine named it the
44th funniest joke of all time.

> I was walking across a bridge one day and I saw a man
> standing on the edge, about to jump off. So I ran over and
> said, "Stop! Don't do it!"
> "Why shouldn't I?" he asked.
> "Well, there's so much to live for."
> "Like what?"
> "Well, are you religious?"
> He said yes.
> I said, "Me too! Are you Christian or Buddhist?"
> "Christian."
> "Me too! Are you Catholic or Protestant?"
> "Protestant."
> "Me too! Are you Episcopalian or Baptist?"
> "Baptist."
> "Wow, me too! Are you Baptist Church of God or Baptist
> Church of the Lord?"
> "Baptist Church of God!"
> "Me too! Are you original Baptist Church of God, or are
> you Reformed Baptist Church of God?"
> "Reformed Baptist Church of God!"
> "Me too! Are you Reformed Baptist Church of God, reformation of 1879, or Reformed Baptist Church of God, reformation of 1915?"

He said, "Reformed Baptist Church of God, reformation of 1915!"

I said, "Die, heretic," and pushed him off.

Besides illustrating just how ridiculous our divisions appear to unbelievers, this joke reveals the dark relationship between group divisions and hostility. Indeed, the message of this joke is consistent with decades of research showing that the mere existence of divisions triggers hostility between groups. However, the numerous Christians who gravitate toward churches that are filled with people who look, talk, worship, think and experience life like them are unaware of the dark side of division. In fact, most people don't see homogeneity as a problem so long as it's not motivated by explicit prejudice. Describing the views of many Christians, Emerson and Smith write, "People are comfortable with different worship styles, want to be with familiar people, and have different expectations about congregations. For these reasons, if congregations end up being . . . homogenous, it is acceptable, if not preferable."

Many of the evangelicals that Emerson and Smith interviewed believed that their desire to remain in a homogenous church had nothing to do with bigotry or intolerance. However, research on group processes shows that group separation and prejudice have a bidirectional relationship—that is, prejudice tends to result in division between groups and division between groups tends to result in prejudice. What begins as seemingly harmless homogeneity often snowballs into distrust, inaccurate perceptions of other groups, prejudice and hostility. Before long and without even knowing it, we become like the man in the joke; we have no problem saying, "Die, heretic" while pushing *them* off the bridge with our words and deeds.

There are many reasons why seemingly innocent group division snowballs into something much darker. One, the simple process of forming a group is a double-edged sword. On the one hand, group formation involves promoting a group identity and engaging in positive behavior toward others in the group. On the other hand, group formation involves going to great lengths to distinguish the group from other groups and ultimately derogating other groups (see chapter 5 for a more in-depth discussion of this idea).

Christians, for example, are fairly good at treating others in their church group well. However, we run into trouble when we're asked to treat Christians who are different from us well, particularly if those Christians violate one of our core values. We seem to have no problem derogating *those* Christians in our blogs, pulpits and tweets. Indeed, research shows that Christians tend to treat fellow group members well and nonmembers poorly. Simply reminding people of their identity as Christians by exposing them to Christian concepts like *Bible, sermon, heaven* and *Messiah* leads them to engage in prosocial behavior, but *only* toward fellow group members. Specifically, after being exposed to Christian concepts, Christians are more prosocial, generous, cooperative, honest and less hypocritical *toward fellow group members.*

Exposure to Christian concepts, however, also increases aggression toward nonmembers, willingness to exact revenge on nonmembers and support for violence toward nonmembers. One would hope that Christians who are reminded of their Christian identity would love *all* others more. However, that is not the case. Being reminded of Christian identity leads people to love their fellow group members well, but hate those who do not share their core values, attitudes and experiences.

This shocking finding is consistent with basic group processes and has everything to do with how we categorize Christians. Humans naturally create group categories that distinguish *us* versus *them.* This distinction is good for group formation; we have a stronger group identity and greater group solidarity when we can easily distinguish ourselves from other groups. However, when it comes to the way we categorize Christians, our natural tendency to make us/them distinctions is complicated by the fact that our fellow church members are mostly, if not entirely, culturally similar others. For this reason, the people who belong to our homogenous church group and interact with us on a regular basis (our "us") are the people with whom we most closely associate the term *Christian*. As a result, we automatically apply the term *Christian* exclusively to "us" and not to the broader, diverse body of Christ. Ultimately, culturally dissimilar Christians are labeled "them" and are treated like the outsiders they are perceived to be. By this point, proclaiming "Die, heretic!" doesn't seem so far-fetched.

We'll address this issue in greater depth in chapter 3. For now, we note that our homogenous churches, though perhaps not sinister in intent, certainly lead to sinister tendencies that inhibit our ability to interact well with other groups in the body of Christ.

Together in the Trinity and the Cross

In spite of my academic understanding of the dark side effects of group processes, I was generally happy to continue worshiping, living, studying and playing with Christians who were just like me. It ensured that my interactions were as tidy and uncomplicated as could be. I could have easily lived my whole life actively avoiding the Wrong Christians in my life or passively avoiding the Christians who were simply different.

But the doctrines of the Trinity and the cross required that I reconsider my exclusive lifestyle of sticking to my "neighborhood" and those who are like me. Basically, to the extent that I accept the work of the cross as my invitation to participate in the self-giving intimacy of the Trinity, I must be prepared to embrace self-giving intimacy with the "other." To partake in the sacrificial love of the Trinity is to participate in sacrificial love with *all* others, not just the ones who are part of my homogenous Christian group.

Theologian Miroslov Volf points out that loving, knowing and embracing Wrong Christian is the only appropriate response to the loving work of the cross: "When God sets out to embrace the enemy, the result is the cross. . . . Having been embraced by God, we must make space for others in ourselves and invite them in— even our enemies. This is what we enact as we celebrate the Eucharist. In receiving Christ's broken body and spilled blood, we, in a sense, receive all those whom Christ received by suffering."

Taking it one step further, Christ's work on the cross eradicates the need for pejorative distinctions between Right Christian and Wrong Christian, tears down the fences between our "neighborhoods" and introduces a whole new reality—one that is marked by a radical standard of unity and reconciliation in the midst of difference. Cain Hope Felder writes, "Because of Christ's blood, all believers are supposed to be transported into a new household of reconciliation and solidarity."

As much as we'd like to believe that Jesus is the author of our Right Christian and Wrong Christian distinctions, we can't because it is simply untrue. By pursuing us with great tenacity in spite of our differences with him, he shows us that he doesn't have need for those distinctions. Jesus pursues us despite theological differences; his theology is more comprehensive and accurate than any of ours. He also pursues us despite cultural differences; he's holy, we're sinful—that's a pretty significant "cultural" difference. Finally, the incarnation is evidence that he pursues us despite physical differences. His actions and words suggest that he is serious about connecting, in spite of physical, cultural and theological differences. I'm reminded of the oft-quoted first and second commandments: to love God and to love our neighbors (Matthew 22:34-40). When Jesus gives us the second commandment, he precisely neglects to mention physical, cultural and theological differences. Raising the stakes, he simply says to love each other. He even tells the story of the good Samaritan in order to redefine what it means to be a neighbor, lest we incorrectly apply the term exclusively to those who are near, familiar and like us—you know, the people with whom it is natural and easy to be neighbors.

A New Reality: The Household of God

Reconciliation scholar Curtiss DeYoung makes the point that relationships between people in the household of God should be radically unifying and inclusive. He writes:

> In the household of faith, our relationship with God takes priority over our relatedness to family, race, culture, nation, gender, or any other group we belong to. This reordering also transforms how we relate to each other. The concept of family was reconstrued in the household of God. The terms *sister, brother, mother, father, friend,* and *neighbor* were all reinterpreted and redefined by Jesus. As Jesus said, "For whoever does the will of my Father in heaven is my brother and sister and mother" (Matthew 12:50). . . . The household of God is an image that beckons the community of Jesus Christ to be a place of convergence for the great rivers of humanity. People of all cultures, races, languages, nations, tribes, and clans reside in the household of faith.

The blueprint of the household of God looks nothing like the blueprints of our own cultural and social cliques. If we want to know how to embody the household of God, we need look no further than to Jesus. While on earth, Jesus modeled this new reality by connecting with every type of person around—conservative theologians, liberal theologians, prostitutes, divorcees, children, politicians, people who party hard, military servicemen, women, lepers, ethnic minorities, celebrities and so forth—and inviting them to be part of his group and to work *together* to bring wholeness to their cracked and crumbling world. After Jesus ascended into heaven, this continued to be his modus operandi for doing miraculous things in the world. It seems as though the early leaders of the church would agree.

Paul, Peter, Luke, John, James and the writer of Hebrews repeatedly and emphatically make the same point: the unified church is the vehicle through which the kingdom of God is powerfully communicated to the world (see Acts 4:32; Romans 16:17; 1 Corinthians 1:10-17; Ephesians 4:1-7, 12-13; Hebrews 2:10-11; 1 Peter 5:5). When Paul talks about our unique gifts and perspectives, he provides a framework within which our differences can be exercised. He sets the standard high by using the framework of the whole body of Christ in which each gift or perspective is simply one part working in concert with all of the other parts under the direction of Christ. Paul's use of the unified physical body as a metaphor for the unified church makes it clear that the unified church must operate at a high level of integration and humble interdependence.

Consider the physical body. Every action we make is the result of a highly integrated web of interdependence that involves communication with and reliance upon multiple parts of the body. If a fly buzzes by and lands on my arm, my sensory neurons in my skin send a message up my spinal cord to my brain via my interneurons (an army of humble internal messenger cells), alerting my brain that a fly has landed on my arm. Once the brain receives this information, it makes an executive decision about how to deal with the fly and then sends multiple coordinated messages (again, via the interneurons) to my motor neurons, who ultimately direct my motor muscles to swat the fly away.

The simple action of swatting a pesky fly requires input and responses from numerous parts of the body that all must work together in order to coordinate the action. More complicated actions require far more interdependent communication.

For example, there are many different kinds of sensory neurons—some that sense smells, others that sense taste, still others that sense sound and so on—that must work together in order to send accurate sensory information to the brain. If this diversity is not effectively coordinated in the body, the body fails to function as it should.

The same is true for Christians. To respond to God's call fully, we need to express our interdependent diversity in individual churches, denominations and organizations as well as in the worldwide body of Christ. We must be connected to those who are different within our respective churches *and* we must be connected to those who are different in the larger body of Christ.

This is the tall order of multilevel unity to which Paul calls us. This degree of unity requires a humble posture that values the perspectives and gifts that other parts offer, recognizes the dire need for interdependence between the parts and accordingly invests significant resources toward connecting with other parts. The homogenous, culturally isolated church, denomination or organization is not truly participating in the body of Christ. The broken and fragmented body needs to be healed. We've lost sight of our framework, and as a result, we are hurting.

The Benefits of a Diverse Body of Christ

Contrary to common beliefs, the body of Christ's diversity is an asset, not a pain in the neck. Research shows that diverse groups are better groups—diverse groups come up with more creative and more effective ideas than groups composed of similar people.

Organizational researchers Bantel and Jackson assessed the diversity of top management teams at 199 banks and found that teams that were more diverse with respect to age, education and length of time on the team were better able to create innovative solutions to administrative challenges. Diverse teams are more creative teams because they can benefit from the wide range of opinions, ideas and resources that diversity offers and apply it to a more thorough discussion of the issue at hand.

Organizational experts also believe that nondiverse groups find it harder to keep learning because each member is bringing less and less unique information to the table. Similar people share similar experiences and acquire similar knowledge, but diverse people differ in their experiences and acquire diverse knowledge. In the end, the diverse group with access to diverse knowledge wins. However, there is one important caveat: Leaders hoping to build diverse teams should be aware that in order to fully utilize the wider range of resources and increased learning that diversity offers, each member of the diverse group must be of equal status. Group members with lower status may lack confidence and express their opinions less frequently. In sum, diverse groups that fully live out the biblical mandate to unite under one household of God will reap the benefits of increased learning, increased creativity and more effective problem solving.

The Trouble with Groupthink

Diverse groups are also less likely to fall prey to groupthink. Groupthink happens when the group members are so pressured into putting forth a united front while making a decision that they fail to voice legitimate differences in opinion. For fear of being perceived as dissenters and abnormal group members, those with different opinions hide their true opinions. Instead, they disingenuously voice agreement with the other group members. In the end, the group makes an uninformed decision that could have greatly benefitted from more thorough discussion and more diverse viewpoints.

Groupthink has a long track record of wreaking havoc on group decisions. It explains the poor decision-making in the Bay of Pigs invasion in 1961 and the pre–World War II decision to ignore a potential Japanese threat to Pearl Harbor. Researchers who study groupthink believe that groups that are mostly composed of similar people and are isolated from other diverse groups are most likely to succumb to groupthink. In other words, the typical homogenous church that has very little meaningful contact with other diverse churches is going to be a sucker for groupthink.

Former Presbyterian minister Gerald Tritle applied research on groupthink to situations involving church leadership teams and found that homogenous and highly cohesive elder boards are especially susceptible to groupthink. Tritle suggests that elder boards are likely inflicted with groupthink if they are suffering from any of the following symptoms:

1. They overestimate their invulnerability or high moral stance.

2. They collectively rationalize the decisions they make.

3. They demonize or stereotype other groups and their leaders.

4. They have a culture of uniformity wherein individuals censor themselves and others so that the façade of group unanimity is maintained.

5. They contain members who take it upon themselves to protect the group leader (usually the pastor) by keeping information—theirs or that of other group members—from that leader.

He ultimately concludes that groupthink produces an inability to "work out theological or ministerial unity" within the larger body of Christ and a "narcissism of small [doctrinal] differences."

According to Tritle, church leadership teams that make decisions in a homogenous vacuum are more likely to make less-informed decisions while perceiving that their decision is superior to those of other groups. The perception that their decision is morally superior to those of other groups gives them license to adopt a narcissistic, defensive and inflexible stance that makes it nearly impossible for them to achieve unity with other cultural groups in the body of Christ. I bet the guy who yelled, "Die, heretic!" in Emo Phillips's joke was on one of the church boards that Tritle studied.

Basically, more diverse groups that are also meaningfully connected to different groups are less likely to make decisions that are influenced by groupthink. In many ways, however, the body of

Christ is broken, and as a result, churches are looking inward rather than outward. They make ill-informed decisions and adopt extreme stances that ultimately decrease their ability to work well with other Christians.

Even more troubling, the fragmentation of the body of Christ is unfolding alongside the unifying forces of globalization and post-modernism. The voices in the world have become increasingly diverse and interconnected; churches should be ready to welcome and engage individuals who represent all aspects of this diversity. Unfortunately, due to cultural isolation, most churches are not in a position to do this well. As churches have maintained and even increased cultural segregation, their ability to operate in and impact the diverse world has diminished. By focusing on their own specific, insular cultures rather than actively welcoming those who lie beyond ethnic, gender, economic, ideological and cultural lines, churches are at great risk of engaging in groupthink as they make decisions on how to best impact society. The more we interact with those who are different, the more we can respond to the needs of those who are different.

The body of Christ is vast, diverse, talented and brimming with resources. I wonder how many real world issues we could tackle if we weren't so busy bickering about the correct way to define a doctrine or which political party is better equipped to solve the crises in our country and beyond. What if we decided that we were going to use our numbers, our expertise and our (potential) unity to solve real problems?

Think about AIDS. I've become acquainted with a modest-sized church in Kigali, Rwanda, that is so committed to bringing relief to HIV/AIDS victims that it is offering practical programs that rival those of the Kigali government. The church is at the center of both social and spiritual change in the city. As if the wow factor isn't high enough, it turns out that the church is composed of members of both the Hutus and Tutsis, two tribes that have a history of being archenemies that climaxed in genocide in 1994. Talk about overcoming hurdles in order to work together and bring about change. What would it look like for the Western church to work together like this? How much could we change? Could we eradicate AIDS? Could we end world hunger? The possibilities are endless.

Of course, this sort of collaboration would require that we discover a way to find unity in the midst of our differences. And that's where it gets tricky. It's guaranteed to be difficult. (That's what the next several chapters are about.) But it's doable. (That's what the chapters after those are about.) As a social psychologist and a member of the church, I hope that our conversation on group processes will help.

Chapter 2 Questions

1. What does your vision of heaven look like? Does it more closely resemble Chicago or the household of God?

2. What are some of the factors that led you to join your church or Christian organization?

3. Think of a time when you "I-shared" with another person. How did that experience affect your relationship with that person?

4. How do shared experiences (or lack thereof) affect your relationships with believers who are very different from you?

5. Do you see evidence of the "snowball effect" in the body of Christ?

6. How might Christians benefit from more interactions with other Christians who are very different from them?

3

Divisions Erected Out of Thin Air

How Categorizing Distorts How We See Each Other

Imagine how much time you would waste each day if you didn't have a concept for chairs. Every time you encountered any object with four legs and a seat, you would examine it, stare at it and wonder whether you were supposed to walk on it, eat it, fear it or sit on it. This would consume a ridiculous amount of your time.

Of course this isn't the case, because you probably categorize all sturdy objects with three or more legs and a seat as chairs. So lots of different varieties of chairs—barstools, Adirondack chairs, highchairs, formal dining room chairs, step stools and so on—are all tossed into your chair category. Anytime you encounter an object that remotely fits your concept of a chair, you automatically know exactly what it is and that you're supposed to sit on it. Case closed.

By categorizing simple objects like chairs, we conserve our limited mental energy. In general, this is a wonderful strategy for coping with the world and all its myriad objects, ideas and patterns of life.

The Cognitive Miser
Social psychologists Shelley Taylor and Susan Fiske coined the term *cognitive miser* to describe our natural tendency to conserve

cognitive resources. The human brain is limited in its ability to pay attention to and process information; the volume of information to which we are exposed on a daily basis far exceeds the brain's ability to process it. To cope with this imbalance, we become cognitive misers, conserving our mental energy by selectively choosing what we'll pay attention to, using mental shortcuts (like categorizing) and avoiding situations that demand a lot of cognitive resources.

We can conserve our valuable and limited cognitive energy by spending time with people who are like us and whose behavior we can easily predict. Conversely, our interactions with people who are different from us or who violate our expectations are laden with uncertainty and are cognitively taxing.

To test this idea, social psychologist Jim Blascovich and colleagues conducted a study in which participants were asked to interact with individuals who either violated or confirmed their expectations. Specifically, the individual who confirmed their expectations was a white person with a strong Southern accent, whereas the individual who violated their expectations was an Asian person with a strong Southern accent. The idea is that white people with strong Southern accents are a dime a dozen. Few Americans would be surprised to encounter such a person. By contrast, Asian people with strong Southern accents are much less common. Consequently, crossing paths with an Asian person with a strong Southern accent would be memorable—and for most people, cognitively taxing.

After interacting with either the Asian person or the white person, participants were asked to complete a cognitive task. As predicted, the participants who interacted with the Asian person with the strong accent performed more poorly on the cognitive task. The researchers concluded that the participants who were required to interact with a person who violated their expectations used a significant amount of their cognitive energy navigating the uncertain social situation. Their cognitive resources were depleted and no longer available for the subsequent cognitive task.

The Cognitive Miser in Me

The summer before my senior year in college, I worked at a camp on Martha's Vineyard, an island off the coast of Massachusetts. The "Vineyard" is a mecca for preppy people. If you go there, prepare yourself to be overwhelmed by seersucker and pastels—or worse, the combination of the two.

During the summer, I became friends with a group of guys who were fraternity brothers at a certain mid-Atlantic university (I would share the name of this university, but I've already antagonized the entire city of Chicago, so I'm going to behave—at least for the time being). Not surprisingly, the frat bros were sharing a summer home on the island. Each of the guys wore similar J. Crew polos and Nantucket red pants, listened to the same music (Phish, Dave Matthews and other preppy-certified bands), had graduated from the same prep school and played the same sport: lacrosse. (What, were you thinking track and field? *Please.* It was either going to be lacrosse or squash.)

By the time I had interacted with these guys for about three minutes, I had reached the conclusion that *all* frat boys from this particular mid-Atlantic university were preppy lacrosse players. Period. It didn't matter that I only knew a fraction of the guys in the fraternity. Based on my limited interaction with a handful of group members, I apparently felt comfortable making assumptions about the rest of the guys in the fraternity. I only needed to know a little bit about the group in order to make sweeping, stereotype-laden generalizations about the group. What can I say? I'm an expert at becoming an expert on groups to which I do not belong.

We're all experts at doing this. No wonder. It's a lot of mental work to treat everyone as an individual instead of just relying on categories.

When Categorizing Helps

We can create categories of groups so easily that we often do it without even thinking. We have a natural ability to do so. We tend to label and categorize just about everything. Historians divide time into eras; biologists classify animals into species; politicians split the so-called United States into blue states and red states. Our minds are designed to do this well, and for the most part, this is a good thing.

Naturally our ability to categorize extends to groups of people. Back in the 1950s, social psychologist Fritz Heider referred to all humans as naive psychologists. Whether we are trained in psychology or not, we have a strong need to make sense of our confusing world so that we can exert control in our lives and make informed choices about the future. We are constantly analyzing situations, trying to predict the behavior of others and attempting to pinpoint answers to complex philosophical questions. However, this way of living requires a great deal of mental energy, which is tricky because as cognitive misers we don't want to waste mental energy! For this reason, we conserve valuable cognitive resources by categorizing individuals into social groups and relying on information about social group membership to help us interact with an individual and predict his or her behavior.

Categorizing can be helpful in many ways. If I walk into a restaurant and am greeted by the host, I can easily make assumptions about the host without utilizing too much cognitive energy. Based on what I know about the social category of "restaurant hosts," I can automatically assume that this specific host in this specific restaurant will ask me how many people are in my party, lead me to a table and so on.

If an individual has been categorized into a group, I already have a preconceived set of expectations and responses at my disposal to help me interact with the individual while conserving my own limited mental energy. Categorizing helps us all to process information in an energy-efficient way. This is why extended periods in a different culture (whether nearby or far away) can be so stressful. If we aren't sure what the social cues are for when we are supposed to laugh, smile, look away, speak, be silent, stand, sit, eat, not eat, arrive, leave, be on time, be late and so on, we are constantly trying to figure out what's expected of us and what certain words and actions mean. The result can be fatigue, anxiety, stress or anger. Once we can see patterns and create categories, our stress levels subside.

When Categorizing Hurts

Categorizing, like all shortcuts, has its drawbacks. Most importantly, in our haste to conserve mental energy we often erect divisions out of thin air by grouping people into smaller homogenous categories. These are typically based on less significant but easily distinguishable features like physical characteristics, language and theology that indicate membership in specific homogenous groups rather than less obvious but more important features that indicate membership in larger diverse groups.

Research on *minimal groups*—groups that are formed based on an inconsequential characteristic such as whether an individual underestimated or overestimated how many marbles were in a jar—suggests that simply putting people into groups (e.g., overestimators and underestimators) increases the likelihood that they will focus on the specific factor that divides them (their estimation tendency) and disregard the more significant factors that unite them (being students at the same university).

By dividing larger categories that are very diverse (such as the body of Christ) into smaller, less diverse subcategories (such as ethnic or denominational groups), we're better able to make assumptions and predictions, thus conserving mental energy. For example, if I come upon a Korean Christian, I can conserve more mental energy if I conceive of this person as a Korean (a relatively smaller and more homogenous group) rather than a member of the body of Christ (a relatively larger and more heterogeneous group). The larger group is too diverse to enable me to make assumptions about the Korean individual's theology, worship style, language, food preferences and so forth. It is significantly more energy-consuming to predict the actions of a member of a large, diverse group because one cannot make as many assumptions about the characteristics, values and tendencies of the group.

As a result, rather than perceiving the body of Christ as one large group, we often perceive numerous distinct groups within the body of Christ; rather than seeing people as distinct individuals within the body of Christ, we often perceive them as nondistinct members of a cultural subgroup. Consequently, the group categories that were intended to help us preserve cognitive energy in our interpersonal interactions actually serve to create unhelpful categorical boundaries between different groups. By focusing on smaller, distinct categories for church groups, we erect and fixate on divisions that are far less important than the larger, diverse group of members of the body of Christ.

No matter how we categorize these distinct church groups (based on beliefs, language, ethnicity, location, age or some other criterion), we typically draw a strong distinction between our *ingroup* and the *outgroup*. The people in our ingroup are those who are obviously like us. The people in the outgroup are those who are obviously not at all like us; they are the "other."

The distinctions that separate one group from another are guarded at all costs because they serve an important function: they provide clear information about how a person should be categorized. If the distinction between two groups becomes blurred, it is more difficult to categorize someone as a member of a certain group and, by extension, to save mental energy by using their membership in a social category to predict their behavior. This helps to explain why we create Right Christian and Wrong Christian labels in the first place, why we are so invested in enforcing them and why they are so rigid. It wouldn't do to have a fuzzy idea of who Wrong Christian is. No, I need a clear idea so I can easily identify him and keep him at bay, so as not to confuse him with all of the Right Christians that I know. For this practical reason, humans have a strong instinct to categorize people based on social group memberships that are considerably homogenous (and thus easy to assess) and also to preserve the rigid boundaries of the social groups.

By simply categorizing, we often create subcategories that detract from the more important, all-inclusive category of the body of Christ. Before we know it, whether people are pro-life or pro-choice, Calvinist or Arminian, or black or white is more important than whether they are part of the family of God. Further, these subcategory distinctions may start out as mere *descriptive* labels (such as pro-life or pro-choice), but they often deteriorate into *value* labels (Right Christian and Wrong Christian) that afford our group higher status.

The simple act of using us/them distinctions leads us to prefer *us* over *them*. Charles Perdue and colleagues found that simply creating distinctions between the ingroup and the outgroup increases bias toward the outgroup. In one experiment, they showed people nonsense syllables (e.g., *xeh*, *yof* and *giw*) that were paired with either pronouns that referred to the ingroup (*us*, *we* or *ours*) or pronouns that referred to the outgroup (*them*, *they* or *theirs*). In other words, people were shown pairings such as "*our xeh*" and "*their giw*" Afterward, they listed each of the nonsense syllables alone and asked participants to rate how "pleasant" each nonsense syllable was. They found that participants rated nonsense syllables that had been paired with pronouns referring to the ingroup as more pleasant than those that had been paired with pronouns referring to the outgroup. Even though the people in the study had no idea what *xeh* was, they were sure that it was more pleasant than *giw* simply because it was associated with their group.

This research suggests that simply distinguishing between *us* and *them* within the body of Christ leads us to like *us* and things associated with *us* more than we like *them* and things associated with *them*. This happens even when we don't really know what we're talking about or haven't humbly listened to the outgroup's point of view. On some level, it's possible that we don't like the way *they* do communion/politics/hermeneutics/worship simply because it's *their* way and not *our* way. It's our way or the highway.

By categorizing, we often erect divisions out of thin air, create distinctions between the ingroup and outgroup, and then attach value to the ingroup but not the outgroup. These are the unintended but sinister side effects of normal categorizing and are, unfortunately, only the beginning.

"We Are Unique; *They* Are the Same"

When we categorize, not only do we draw a very clear line between those who are like us and those who are not like us, but we also tend to think that all of the people who are not like us are the same. It's not just that they are all different from us; they are all different *in the same way*.

The fancy name for this tendency is the *outgroup homogeneity effect*. On the one hand, we tend to view the outgroup as homogenous: "*They* are all the same." On the other hand, we tend to view our ingroup as heterogeneous: "*We* are all unique." Once we reach this conclusion (and we do so quite swiftly), we are no longer motivated to interact with and learn about the outgroup. We think we already know everything there is to know about them.

The outgroup homogeneity effect is surprisingly common. A couple of years ago, one of my undergraduate research assistants introduced me to a popular but controversial book called *Stuff White People Like*. It's essentially a primer on white culture stereotypes in which the author, a white guy named Christian Lander, dispenses satirical advice on how nonwhite people can impress their white friends. For example, Lander lists "outdoor performance clothes" as stuff white people like and adds:

The main reason white people like these clothes is that they allow them to believe that at any moment they could find themselves with a Thule rack on top of their car headed to a national park. It could be 4:00 p.m. on a Saturday when they might get the call: "Hey, man, you know what we need to do? Kayak then camping, right now. I'm on my way to get you. There is no time to change clothes."

Though it is unlikely that they will ever receive this call, white people hate the idea of missing an opportunity to enjoy outdoor activities just because they weren't wearing the right clothes.

If you plan on spending part of your weekend with a white person, it is strongly recommended that you purchase a jacket or some sort of "high-performance" T-shirt, which is like a regular shirt, just a lot more expensive.

Lander's list of stuff white people like also includes unpaid internships, religions their parents don't belong to, *Arrested Development*, ugly Christmas sweater parties, Wes Anderson movies, basketball assists and microbreweries.

The satirical humor in *Stuff White People Like* heavily relies on the outgroup homogeneity effect. It overflows with stereotypes and banks on the fact that the reader will recognize the caricatures, chuckle to herself, nod in agreement and say: "Yes, this is how *all* white people are. They are all the same." According to research on the outgroup homogeneity effect, nonwhite people (outgroup members), on the one hand, should be more likely to make this assumption, which is convenient given that the tongue-in-cheek book is supposedly written for nonwhite people. On the other hand, white people (ingroup members) should be more likely to note the vast differences among white people. "*I'm* not like that," white people might insist. Or, "Not *all* white people are like that," they might say.

The outgroup homogeneity effect doesn't just concern ethnic

minorities. Social psychologists have found that people from China, Vietnam and Japan perceive themselves as distinct from one another, but many Westerners have a tough time telling them apart. Liberals lump together all conservatives. Drama majors like to talk about "math types" and math majors like to talk about "drama types." Californians brag about their cultural and ethnic diversity while non-Californians talk of the "typical Californian." And old people tend to think that all young people are the same.

In one of many experiments on the outgroup homogeneity effect, Patricia Linville asked elderly adults and college-aged students to describe their age ingroup and age outgroup. For example, Linville asked college-aged participants to share their perceptions of both college-aged students (their age ingroup) and elderly adults (their age outgroup). She found that college-aged adults tended to see themselves as belonging to a heterogeneous group—they were easily able to talk about the subtle and obvious differences among college-aged adults. However, they perceived elderly adults as homogenous. They described older adults in simplistic terms such as "grandmothers," "nursing home residents" and "travelers." Essentially, they thought that all elderly adults were the same.

It would be easy to chalk this up to youthful ignorance. *Of course, self-centered college kids think that all old people are the same*, we older adults say to ourselves with smug satisfaction. However, elderly adults showed the same pattern. They perceived themselves as heterogeneous and college-aged students as homogeneous. In fact, elderly adults primarily described college-aged students in equally simplistic and homogenous ways, including "party animals," "athletes" and "fraternity or sorority types." It appears as though old people fall prey to the outgroup homogeneity effect too.

It's easy to see how the outgroup homogeneity effect can bias our perceptions of other followers of Christ and prevent us from leaving our comfortable groups. Not only do we overlook valuable information about a group's variability, but we also think we know everything about them. We are certain that all of the women in the conservative church on the other side of town are pregnant and barefoot even though we have not yet gotten to know any of the members of the church (or their many homeschooled children).

Speaking of homeschoolers, we are certain that they all are weird and socially awkward (this homeschooled author is no exception). We are certain that all of the men who belong to the church with the female lead pastor are weak and need to listen to more Mark Driscoll sermons. We are certain that all students at Christian colleges are obsessed with getting married. We are certain that all the people at a particular church vote the same way. We are certain that all the people at the Pentecostal church are raging Pentecostals with over-developed sensory systems and underdeveloped theology.

"I Know What They Think"

I recently worked with a predominantly white Christian organization that was attempting to address its poor track record of attracting and retaining ethnically diverse participants. Before we implemented any "diversity" programs, I suggested that we first survey the few people of color who had recently interacted with the organization in order to assess their perceptions of the organization. Once we had the feedback in hand, we could use it to devise an effective plan for organizational change that would address the diversity challenges.

When the white leader of the organization heard my suggestion, however, he scoffed, "Why bother spending resources on collecting data from people of color? I can probably tell you what they're thinking."

How can a white leader of an organization that admittedly does not have a successful history of engaging people of color honestly think that he can estimate the rich and varied perspectives of people of color without even talking to them? The answer is simple: because he had succumbed to the outgroup homogeneity effect. He did not perceive the outgroup's perspective as rich, varied and absolutely crucial to the organization's success. Rather, he perceived it as homogenous and simple—so simple that he thought he could address the diversity problem without help from any diverse people.

Perceptions of outgroup homogeneity often lead to prejudice. By perceiving the ingroup as heterogeneous and the outgroup as homogenous, group members are less likely to believe that their group would benefit from more diversity, more likely to perceive the outgroup in unflattering and oversimplified ways, and more likely to believe that the outgroup has very little to offer them. Thanks to the outgroup homogeneity effect, our perceptions of outgroups tend to be inaccurate and arrogant—not exactly a winning combination.

What We Think They Think of Us

I recently attended a unity dinner and worship service that was cohosted by a traditionally black church and a predominantly white evangelical church. From the seating arrangements to a carefully devised schedule to the diversity of the leadership team, the church leaders who spearheaded the event went to great lengths to design an event that would encourage the two groups to engage in meaningful crosscultural interactions.

Despite their hard work, all of the white people ended up mingling on one side of the room and all of the black people ended up mingling on the other side of the room. Even though both groups were physically present in the same room, an invisible but immovable barrier stood between them.

Why do people who have a heart for unity have such a hard time actually uniting? This question has befuddled pastors and church leaders who have attempted to build bridges across cultural lines but have faced an unyielding barrier of division. An understanding of *metaperceptions*—what we think they think of us—can help us see the forces that lead us to stick to our own kind and keep us from sauntering over to the other side of the room in order to connect with different people.

It turns out that categorizing also influences metaperceptions. While perceptions are the way we view our ingroup and outgroup, *meta*perceptions (in this case) are the way that we think the outgroup views our ingroup. When it comes to groups getting along or not, *what we think of them* is just as important as *what we think they think of us*. If we miscalculate others' perceptions of us, we're far more likely to misunderstand them when we actually do cross paths. Unfortunately, research shows that our metaperceptions are wrought with miscalculations. Most importantly, our metaperceptions tend to be overly pessimistic; we tend to believe that what they think of us is far worse than what they actually think.

For example, research has shown that women think men are judging them more negatively than men actually are, and vice versa. Further, opposing gender groups often wrongly believe that the other group does not desire contact with them when the opposite is true. Even groups based on socioeconomic and ethnic differences tend to overestimate how negatively other groups view them.

When different church groups are invited to interact, they often assume that the other group does not really want to get to know them when in fact this is probably an incorrect assumption. If both groups are plagued by inaccurate metaperceptions, neither group will actively engage the other; instead they will stick to their own groups. The invisible forces of metaperceptions can thwart even well-planned, well-intentioned unity events, leaving leaders shaking their heads and wondering what went wrong as the two groups still passively resist meaningful crosscultural interaction.

One reason why this scenario is so common is that inaccurate metaperceptions go hand in hand with perceptions of outgroup homogeneity to form a dynamic and divisive duo. If we assume that we already know what they are like, then we can assume that we already know what they think of us. Unfortunately, in tandem, our perceptions of outgroup homogeneity and our metaperceptions lead us to believe with a degree of certainty that the other group doesn't like us and doesn't want to interact with us. This results in further divisions and infrequent meaningful interactions.

These perceptual problems exist because we tend to spend the majority of our time with fellow members of our most relevant ingroups. Spending time with the people who are part of our lives isn't necessarily a bad thing. However, since there are only so many hours in the day, we end up spending very little time with outgroup members. As a result, we gather large and varied amounts of information about ingroup characteristics, like how diverse and open-minded we are, and remain relatively less informed about outgroup characteristics, like how diverse and open-minded they are.

In spite of our obvious lack of interaction with many outgroups in the church, we tend to think of ourselves as experts on these groups. We already know what *they* are like, we tell ourselves. Further, we already know that they don't like us. So *what we think of them* and *what we think they think of us* continue to go unchallenged. Ultimately, we maintain our distance from what we perceive to be the homogenous and less interesting outgroup and stick to the groups of people we are familiar with and whom we perceive to be far more nuanced and evolved than everyone else.

When Categorizing Taints the Past, Present and Future

Once acquired, inaccurate perceptions and metaperceptions begin to take on lives of their own by overriding objective reality and distorting our interpretations and memories.

Try an exercise with me. Get a pen and a piece of paper. Then read the following list out loud:

bed

rest

awake

tired

dream

night

blanket

doze

slumber

snore

pillow

peace

yawn

drowsy

Now put this book aside and write down as many of the words as you can remember. (No cheating!)

How many words were you able to list? Did you recall *pillow*? *doze*? *sleep*? *peace*? *blanket*? If you think you recalled *sleep*, you have been hoodwinked by categorization processes, because *sleep* was not on the original list. However, all of the words in the list are probably categorized with your concept for sleep. As a result, simply thinking about these sleep-related words evoked your concept for sleep. Without knowing it, you relied on your category for sleep-related words to help you recall the list. Cognitive psychologists Kathleen McDermott and Henry Roediger have created several tests just like this one to demonstrate the ways in which categories can lead people to misremember information or events.

My friend and mentor Stan Klein has also spent a significant amount of time researching this process. A few years back, Stan conducted a study in El Paso, Texas, a city that boasts a significant Hispanic community. Given what we know about categories and how easily they are created, it's probably safe to say that the citizens of El

Paso who participated in Stan's study had created a category for the Hispanics in the city. Whether this category was filled with accurate information is a completely different question. Nevertheless, Stan wanted to know how this particular category would affect people's memories, particularly when their memories were hazy.

He asked the participants in his study to read a story about a person named X who was living in El Paso. Among other things, the story mentioned that X was young, that X was a vandal and that X spent a lot of time with friends after school. Twenty minutes after the participants had finished reading the story, they were asked to recall whether X was a vandal. The vast majority (87%) of participants answered correctly: yes, X did vandalize. Next, participants were asked to recall whether X was Hispanic, male and in a gang. About half of participants incorrectly recalled that X was Hispanic even though there was no mention of ethnicity in the story. In addition, about 80% incorrectly recalled that X was male even though there was no mention of sex in the story. Further, about 40% incorrectly believed that X was a gang member even though there was no mention of gang activity in the story.

When participants were asked to recall specific information about X, they recalled a detailed, stereotypic version of X that was based on their category of Hispanics, rather than what was actually stated in the story. One day later, Stan called each of the participants and asked them the exact same questions about X. He found that this time around, *almost all* of the participants incorrectly recalled that X was Hispanic, male and in a gang.

For better or for worse, we use the contents of our categories to fill in the holes when we're asked to recall information. The hazier our recollection, the more we rely on what we think we know about the category in order to make judgments. Again, this is not necessarily a bad thing. Sometimes categories can help us to easily and accurately interpret and recall information. Other times, as in the instance of Stan's study, the categories completely override objective reality and lead us to interpret and recall situations inaccurately. We have a tendency to remember what we want to remember, whether it is accurate or not.

Unfortunately, the fact that we tend to interpret and remember information in ways that are consistent with our categories only serves to reaffirm categories that perhaps need to be reevaluated. It's tough to revise our inaccurate categories when we're constantly interpreting information in ways that confirm them. Before long, we've created inflexible categories within which the outgroup is trapped.

In the story of the good Samaritan, Jesus wisely addressed our tendency to cling to rigid and oversimplified categories. Jesus' target audience—Jewish people living in Israel—had an unflattering and oversimplified category for Samaritans that Jesus challenged when he described a Samaritan who didn't fit within the boundaries of the category. By showcasing the ways in which the Samaritan hero violated the Jews' expectations, Jesus was drawing conscious attention to an inaccurate Samaritan category that had probably gone unchallenged for generations. In doing so, Jesus was asking his listeners to reevaluate their Samaritan category. Similarly, I think he's asking us to reevaluate our rigid categories of different groups in the body of Christ.

The sinister side effects of categorizing—erecting divisions between *us* and *them*, thinking that *they* are all the same, automatically thinking that *they* think poorly of *us*, recalling false memories of them, and inaccurately interpreting their behavior—are reinforcing the divide between different church groups. These processes need to be overcome in order to create meaningful interactions between different groups that break down unbiblical and unloving divisions.

From Cognitive Miserliness to Cognitive Generosity

You might be thinking to yourself, *Well, that was depressing. What am I supposed to do now?* Before you sink despairingly into your chair, let me share with you some steps that you can take to lead others and yourself toward unity.

It turns out that the cognitive processes that I described in this chapter are most powerful when they are hidden from view, when they are outside our conscious awareness. Once individuals become consciously aware of these processes—as you just have, by reading this chapter—the processes begin to lose their power. If you are motivated to override them, you absolutely can.

As research shows, once we sincerely believe that inaccurate perceptions are in fact wrong and should be overridden, it's actually possible to do so. Using a test called the implicit attitude test, Keith Payne found that American participants of varied races automatically associate black men with violence and white men with nonviolence—when people are shown pictures of black men, they quickly assume that they are violent, but when people are shown pictures of white men, they quickly assume that they are nonviolent. Sadly, this is the default perception; it's simply a natural byproduct of the way that black and white men are categorized in Western society. However, Payne found that when participants believed that their bias against black men should be suppressed and were motivated to suppress it, they did not associate black men with violence any more than they associated white men with violence. In fact, they were able to do this with relative ease by taking a moment to stop, evaluate their automatic inaccurate perception and revise it. This is good news!

We must relentlessly attack inaccurate perceptions in our everyday interactions, weekly sermons, denominational meetings and dinner table conversations. Now that we are aware that categorizing is polluting our perceptions of other groups in the body of Christ, we must do the work of purifying our perceptions. What we need to do is really quite simple: rather than continuing on as cognitive misers who lazily rely on inaccurate categories to perceive others, we need to engage in what my friend Reverend Jim

Caldwell calls *cognitive generosity*. We need to turn off autopilot and take the time to honestly examine our polluted perceptions.

I do this periodically by making a list of different cultural groups and writing down what I think (what I really think, not what I would ideally like to think) about them. Once I've named the specific biases that I hold, I can be on the lookout for them as I go about my day. When I'm tempted to think or speak one of the biases on my list, I can stop, name it as a bias and not a truth, and correct it. Typically, statements about other groups that begin with "They all . . ." or that have a decidedly sarcastic tone are bias-laden statements. I've found that it's helpful for me to share my list of biases with close friends so that they can speak up if they find me perceiving others inaccurately.

The Power of Unifying Language

As leaders, we must go beyond simply naming and addressing our own biased perceptions or leading the members of our congregations and organizations in naming and addressing their biases. We must also take active steps to expand our category of *us* so that *they* are now included in *us*. We've learned that the mere act of categorizing Christian groups into smaller, homogenous groups that pit *us* against *them* leads us to devalue, misperceive and distance ourselves from them. In order to overcome the consequences of categorizing, we need to address the categorizing problem at its root: the us/them distinctions. We need to rid ourselves of us/them distinctions and lead others in ridding themselves of us/them distinctions. We can start to do this by talking about ourselves differently.

Language significantly affects how we see ourselves and others. In my group identity research, my colleagues and I often take a group of three people who have had no previous contact with each other and attempt to transform their identities as individuals into identities as group members. One significant way in which we do this is by asking them to create a name for their group. Once they acquire a group name, we only refer to them by their group name for the duration of the five-week study; we never, ever refer to them by their individual names. For example, over the course of a one-hour lab session, they hear the experimenter refer to them by their team name approximately fifteen times. Interestingly, by the third or fourth week of the study, we have found that when participants are asked to spontaneously describe themselves, they often include their group name! Even though their group name was unknown to them less than a month before, it has now impacted their identity so much that they use it to describe themselves. Language powerfully shapes the way we think of ourselves.

In the same way that my colleagues and I use language to shape the identity of the participants in our experiments, we can use it to reshape our perceptions of ourselves and other groups in the body of Christ. By default, we often use the terms *us* and *them* when we think about and talk about different church groups.

If we begin to use inclusive language such as *we* and *us* (rather than *they* and *them*) when we refer to the different groups in the body of Christ, we will begin to associate the different groups with the same positive attributes and feelings that we associate with ourselves. Remember the study in which nonsense syllables were paired with ingroup pronouns like *we* or outgroup pronouns like *them*? The people in the study automatically liked the nonsense syllables that were paired with *we* more than the nonsense syllables paired with *them*. When something is part of *us*, we like it more. When different groups in the body of Christ are part of *us*, we like them more.

What if there were no *them* in the body of Christ? What if all were simply *we*? Divisions would begin to weaken. To start, we would stifle the negative effects of categorizing and begin to see others in a more accurate light. Also, by relinquishing divisive us/them distinctions and adopting inclusive "we" language, we would begin to treat different members of the body of Christ like we tend to treat ourselves—graciously, generously and lovingly.

As a bonus, we would also begin to build bridges with different members of the body of Christ. By referring to other group members as *us*, we would implicate ourselves whenever we decide to offer constructive criticism to the other group. No longer would we perceive the problems of other groups in the body of Christ as solely *their* problems. As newly minted members of *us*, their problems are now our problems. We can no longer stand at a distance, point our fingers at them and shake our heads in disgust. We must lovingly and wisely engage because to fail to do so would only hurt ourselves. In this way, consciously avoiding us/them distinctions in the body of Christ changes the way that we approach and perceive each other.

Similarly, if we choose to refer to our brothers and sisters from different groups as members of *us*, we will begin to see them in a more positive light and will take notice of their positive traits. This is a departure from the norm; individuals have a heightened sensitivity to negative information, particularly when it comes to different others. However, the language that we choose to use can overpower the norm. Research shows that the mere use of the word *we* leads individuals to recognize positive words and traits more quickly. When we refer to former outgroup members as *we*, we are more inclined to pay attention to their positive traits. As a result, we are more inclined to draw near to each other, rather than separate.

This way of thinking and speaking is a stark departure from our current way of thinking. As we start to understand more of the hidden forces that divide us, we will begin to adopt a new way of thinking about and relating to other members of the body of Christ.

Chapter 3 Questions

1. Humans categorize all of the time. When do you see this helping you? When do you see it hurting you?

2. Do you find it difficult to see people from other Christian groups first and foremost as fellow members of the body of Christ? Why/why not?

3. Do you think that it's possible to use us/them distinctions between different Christian groups without valuing one group over the other? Why/why not?

4. How do you see the outgroup homogeneity effect ("We are unique; *they* are the same") contributing to divisions in the church?

5. How do you see inaccurate metaperceptions (what we think they think of us) contributing to divisions in the church?

6. What would it take for you to interact with other members of different groups in the body of Christ in a cognitively generous way?

7. How would being more cognitively generous change your thoughts and feelings toward different groups in the body of Christ?

4

Beyond Perceptions

*How Categorizing Pollutes
Our Interactions with Each Other*

During my first year in college, I attended a weekly Bible study that was led by a domineering upperclassman who seemed to be majoring in history and minoring in rebuking me. At the time, he was a staunch Calvinist who thought that my theology was incorrect. He was constantly pointing out that my interpretation of certain Scripture passages was incorrect, that I should switch churches and begin attending his church, that I must do X, Y and Z in order to become a better disciple (of Christ, I presume; it wasn't always clear to me).

The whole situation was intense, and I began to resent him. Unfortunately, since he was the only Calvinist that I knew at the time, I began to create a category for Calvinists based on my (likely inaccurate) perceptions of him: Calvinists were smug, quick to rebuke unsuspecting and innocent first-year students, and convinced that everyone should attend their churches. That pretty much summed up my not-so-insightful perception of Calvinists. Once I had formed a category about the group, the category greatly affected my future interactions.

One day I crossed paths with a different Calvinist, and while introducing herself, she flashed a bright smile at me. You would think that based on my positive interaction with this particular Calvinist, I would have revised my category and stopped believing that they were all smug people. On the contrary, I immediately thought to myself, *Look at that smug smile she just gave me. They are so smug.* My inaccurate category lived on and continued to taint my future interactions with Calvinists.

Thanks to grace and an understanding of group categorizing, I have since reevaluated my category for this group. But we all have a tendency to cling to rigid and oversimplified categories of other groups and this certainly affects how we interact with each other.

"Don't Confuse *Us* with *Them*"

Unfortunately, the tendency to cling to rigid and oversimplified categories of other groups quickly leads us to exaggerate differences between *us* and *them*. We want to be perceived as different from *them* so we exaggerate our differences with the other group.

Here's how it happens. As I mentioned earlier, a natural by-product of categorizing is that we automatically create distinctions between the ingroup and the outgroup. In fact, we often distinguish ourselves from other groups even when there's no logical reason to do so. I recently conducted an experiment on team motivation. For five consecutive weeks, seventy-five three-person teams came into my lab on a weekly basis to compete in an anagram tournament. During the first week of the study, the three members of each team were introduced to each other (they hadn't met before they came into the lab) and were asked to agree on a team name and create a team banner bearing their team name.

Interestingly, the mere process of assigning individuals to groups led them to adopt ingroup categories that distinguished them from outgroups. For example, one team chose to call itself "The Anti-Athletics" only after noticing that another team had named itself the "Sporty Spice Girls." Similarly, one team named itself "The McDreamy Fan Club" (based on a character on the television show *Grey's Anatomy*) and posted their banner proudly on the wall. The next team that came into the lab saw the banner and promptly named itself "The McSteamy Fan Club" (based on Mc-Dreamy's rival character on *Grey's Anatomy*). The teams chose to define themselves in opposition to other teams even though they had not yet met any of the other teams. We tend to do this effortlessly and without much thought.

Whether the distinctions are meaningful or not, we're inclined to move toward one extreme in order to further distinguish ourselves from the outgroup. Above all, *we* don't want to be confused with *them*. By maintaining the boundaries between groups, we're better able to conserve our mental energy by relying on group categories to make decisions. The more we can distinguish our ingroup from the various outgroups, the more easily we can categorize individuals into fellow group members or nonmembers. At this point, our priority becomes distancing ourselves from the other group so that we can maintain the boundaries of our überimportant categories. This often means glossing over common interests and characteristics that could bring us closer to other groups.

Within the political arena, liberals become extremely liberal, exaggerate differences between the liberals and conservatives, and ignore commonalities between liberals and conservatives, and vice versa. This is done with the goal of distinguishing themselves. As the groups distance themselves from each other, the divide between the two categories widens. This process helps everyone to know who is an ally (an ingroup member) and who is an enemy (an outgroup member) in an energy-efficient way.

I often see this process unfolding in the body of Christ. My church in Minneapolis is a curious place. It's a hipster church that's trying to be multiethnic. It's ironic. The church is heavily populated with underemployed videographers and web designers, serves organic, fair-trade coffee in the café, is led by young male and female co-pastors and has *awesome* graphic design. The funny thing is that there's another church just six blocks down the street that's basically just like our church. Lots of hipsters, trying to be multiethnic, lots of unemployed "artists," fair-trade coffee, young male and female co-pastors, similar theology and worship style and *awesome* graphic design. However, if you discuss the blatant similarities with anyone from my church or the other church, you'll hear eerily similar sentiment: "Don't confuse us with them; *we* are *nothing* like *them*." This notion is typically supported by ridiculous arguments such as, "The male co-lead pastor at one church is better looking than the male co-lead pastor at the other church. That's what makes the two churches different." *Oh, okay. Now that you've pointed that out, I can see that the churches are totally different.*

Similarly, I once heard a pastor sum up his reasons for keeping a rival church at bay by saying, "They do communion differently than we do." When we really want to differentiate ourselves from other church groups, we will find any old reason to draw a line in the sand.

Fixating on differences leads us to ignore glaring commonalities and focus on distinguishing ourselves from other groups, making it less likely for us to think that we should get to know other groups and collaborate with them. Even though the process I just described seems somewhat benign, it can lead to destructive consequences.

If the members of two almost identical hipster churches located in the same neighborhood are naturally inclined to focus on minute differences and downplay obvious similarities, what can we expect from Christians who actually differ in significant ways? How would an English-speaking church interact with a Mandarin-speaking church? How would an Episcopal church interact with an evangelical megachurch? How would a traditional black church interact with a predominantly white Presbyterian church? How would a liberal Christian church interact with a conservative Christian church? If we're not on our guard, these invisible forces will lead us to focus more on distinguishing ourselves from other groups than on celebrating the many things we have in common.

This natural inclination to obsess over the characteristics that distinguish our group from other groups is exacerbated by the fact that we spend the majority of our time with fellow group members who confirm our beliefs, culture and way of life. The only people who are contributing to the important conversations of our lives are the people who already happen to agree with us! As a result, we're likely to adopt more extreme and inflexible opinions about our way of doing things. For example, when the only people who are chiming in on our conversations about communion are the people who already think that our way of doing communion is best, we can easily reach the conclusion that our communion practices are un-equivocally right. At that point, it's not much of a stretch for us to believe that another church's different (read: wrong) communion practices are grounds for keeping that church at bay.

"We Are the Gold Standard"

Exaggerating differences also gives way to wider differences in viewpoints. This is called *perspective divergence*—or what I call the *gold standard effect*—and is one of the main causes of divisions be-tween groups. Basically, the gold standard effect leads us to believe that not only are we different from them, but we are also better than them. This is how it works.

When we adopt a unique group identity and surround ourselves with similar ingroup members, we essentially create our own al-ternate universe in which we believe that the standards, ideals and goals of our ingroup should become the new "normal"—not only for our specific subgroup but for the entire larger group, including the outgroup.

Since we think that our way of doing things is the most normal, we interact with others while thinking that our alternate universal laws and way of life are the gold standard for the larger group. Essentially, we begin to believe that we are the model citizens of the larger group and that other subgroups can only hope to be as relevant and valuable as we are.

This particular attitude powerfully widens the divide between groups in the body of Christ because each group believes that they're better members of the body of Christ than individuals in other groups. However, inevitably we must cross paths with the other subgroups in the body of Christ. These interactions are often doomed from the start because we are operating under the laws of our alternate universe and the other group members are operating under the laws of their own alternate universe.

We can't understand why the language, opinions, actions and characteristics of other Christian subgroups are so different from ours. We also can't understand why they think that they know what is best for the body of Christ when *clearly* the opposite is true. We each have our own perspective on the situation, and our perspectives are very different.

Research suggests that the gold standard effect can lead to serious misunderstandings. Thomas Kessler, Amélie Mummendey and their colleagues have discovered that each subgroup within a larger group perceives that its unique characteristics are prototypical for the larger group. In other words, we think that our ingroup represents the best, most important and most typical characteristics of the larger group.

These researchers found that high school teachers and elementary school teachers show signs of the gold standard effect. High school teachers perceive their fellow high school teachers to better represent teachers as a large group than elementary school teachers do. Not to be outdone, elementary school teachers believe that their fellow elementary school teachers better represent teachers than high school teachers.

Even hobby groups show the same pattern: sport bikers think that their group represents the gold standard for the larger group of motorcyclists, but chopper bikers think that their group represents the gold standard. Research also suggests that the gold standard effect can cause serious misunderstandings between groups. Kessler and Mummendey found that sport bikers believed that chopper bikers possessed biased perceptions of sport bikers, and vice versa. Not surprisingly, if chopper bikers inaccurately believe that they best represent the larger group of bikers, they are also likely to believe that sport bikers are not model group members and that their perspective and needs are not relevant. As a result, sport bikers become marginalized group members who are typically disrespected and devalued and must fight for their rightful place among the other motorcyclists.

It is relatively easy to see how the gold standard effect contributes to misunderstanding and division between members of the body of Christ today. I recently met with two pastors—a black man who pastored a predominantly black urban church and a white man who pastored a predominantly white suburban church— who had recently failed at their attempt to lead their churches in working together on a project at the black urban church.

The joint venture began well but soon ended quite poorly, leaving behind a trail of distrust, negative emotions and bruised egos. After hearing each pastor's perspective on the situation, I saw that both pastors were guilty of falling prey to the gold standard effect, particularly when it came to leadership ideals. Each pastor possessed very different ideals about what a leader does and does not do. Further, each pastor projected his ideals onto the other pastor and negatively evaluated him based on criteria that pertained to those ideals. Essentially, each pastor gave the other a failing grade on leadership because they had very different criteria for evaluating leadership, criteria they thought were clearly superior. Neither pastor was aware of the way the gold standard effect was affecting his evaluation of the other pastor, and consequently, neither had thought to address their difference in leadership ideals.

Once we were able to uncover their differences in leadership ideals, the pastors could seek to understand each other's perspectives and work toward healing. If two church groups believe that they best represent the larger body of Christ and automatically require the other group to live up to their unspoken standard, they can easily misunderstand and devalue the other group's viewpoint.

These dynamics lead to disastrous crosscultural interactions. Not only do we distance ourselves from our group's rivals, we also have the audacity to think our increasingly extreme opinions, unique characteristics and distanced group members wholly and accurately represent the larger group. In this way, different groups are further marginalized because they are perceived as "out of touch" and "incompetent." Meanwhile, we are convinced that we have a perfect grasp on reality.

It's difficult to imagine a scenario in which two groups who have succumbed to the gold standard effect can avoid conflict, much less be united.

"Not Listening!"

One serious consequence of the division caused by thinking "Don't confuse *us* with *them*" and "We are the gold standard" is that we are no longer willing to receive much-needed information from outgroup members. Research shows that people are unlikely to receive information from outgroup members, even if the information would help them successfully complete a difficult task.

In one study, Dominic Abrams and his colleagues divided groups of participants into smaller groups based on trivial categories (e.g., groups based on numbers that were randomly assigned to them). Then participants were asked to complete a difficult perceptual task while receiving helpful information from members of either their ingroup or outgroup. They found that participants did not rely on input from outgroup members even when it would have been useful for them to do so. Instead, they toiled on alone. Abrams and colleagues wrote, "[Participants] resisted information purely on the basis that it was derived from a category of person to which they did not belong."

Unfortunately, many members of the body of Christ are as stubborn as the participants in Abrams's study. This is why we rarely make the effort to actively engage in crosscultural interactions. Due to the sinister side effects of categorizing, we don't think that we need information from other groups in the body of Christ; from our perspective, we have everything that we need and if we do need something, we are not inclined to look for it among the groups that lie beyond the boundaries of our own comfortable world.

The sinister effects of normal categorizing—inaccurate perceptions, inaccurate metaperceptions, false interpretations and memories, group polarization and perspective divergence—are working to maintain homogenous church groups and widen the divide between different church groups. These processes need to be overcome in order to begin to create meaningful interactions between differing groups and ultimately break down unbiblical divisions.

The brilliant and challenging metaphor of the body of Christ preaches the need to engage in crosscultural relationships because other groups are our lifelines. If each of our church groups represents one part of the body, it follows that we need to remain connected to each other in order to receive the information and nourishment required for survival. If the hand doesn't stay connected to the rest of the body, it dies and rots. Only a stubborn hand would venture away from its source of life. This analogy can be applied to groups.

Different groups in the body of Christ hold life-giving information. But once they have become the casualties of categorizing processes, relegated to outgroup status and perceived as different or even out of touch, we are not likely to accept their input and help. When we make ingroup/outgroup distinctions within the body of Christ, we cut ourselves off from other parts of the body that may look different, act different and hold divergent perspectives but without which we cannot survive. We are a dismembered body that must overcome categorizing processes in order to become whole again.

What Now?

At the end of chapter 3, I suggested using inclusive language to break down ingroup/outgroup distinctions. Similarly, we can use language to fight against our tendency to exaggerate differences between *us* and *them*. We can do this by intentionally and verbally emphasizing shared characteristics rather than differences—in our small group discussions, from our pulpits and in casual conversations. Groups that are aware of their similarities tend to like each other more. This is why we often form groups with people who seem similar to us in terms of race, culture, lifestyle and so on. However, as we know, our tendency to exaggerate differences between groups causes great divisions and leads us to believe that the divisions are legitimate. One way to reverse this effect is by consciously choosing to highlight shared characteristics in our preaching, conversations and thoughts.

Social identity researcher Richard Crisp found that participants who were asked to think of shared characteristics between the ingroup and outgroup were more likely to rate outgroup members more positively. Interestingly, he found this to be especially true for participants who recognized that their subgroup identity was not as important as the common identity (that included the outgroup). This research suggests that if Christians focus on similarities between themselves and culturally different Christians *and* keep in mind that their identity as Christians is more important than other cultural identities, then they should naturally begin to like culturally different Christians.

Overcoming the Gold Standard Effect:
Taking a Walk in the Outgroup Member's Shoes

Clearly, church groups that wish to achieve crosscultural unity must find a way to neutralize the gold standard effect. And thankfully, the solution to the problem is relatively simple (although time-consuming). Last week I spoke to a group of predominantly white pastors from a predominantly white denomination. During the Q&A, one of the audience members asked me what he could do to better understand some of the challenges that the small number of people of color in the denomination might experience. My answer was simple: in addition to simply asking people of color to share their personal experiences, majority group members should make a habit of going out of their way to "walk a mile" in the shoes of people of color.

Specifically, I encouraged the white men in the room to begin by attending a large, predominantly African American pastors' conference in order to experience what it's like to be one of the few "others" for whom the conference was clearly not designed. By doing this, in one small way, they can begin to understand what it's like to be the "other" who is marginalized and whose perspective is often overlooked and devalued. In other words, they can begin to understand what it's like to be a person of color in their mostly white denomination.

If we never leave our cultural comfort zones, we will continue to be terrorized by the gold standard effect. As members of the largest racial group in America, who are also heavily involved in a predominantly white organization, the white pastors to whom I was speaking can easily go their entire lives without ever knowing what it's like to be a person of color. As a result, a white pastor's reality (which is informed by personal experiences as a majority member) is likely to be extremely different from a black pastor's reality (which is informed by personal experiences as a person of color). If the pastors attempt to form a crosscultural relationship without taking each other's perspective, they will fail. We must seek to understand each other's unique experiences.

Several research studies show that the simple exercise of taking the perspective of an outgroup member can powerfully break down the divisions constructed by the gold standard effect. According to prejudice researcher James Weyant, perspective-taking involves attempting to imagine oneself in another person's shoes, thinking from the other person's point of view, envisioning oneself in the other person's circumstances and feeling what the other person is feeling. One study asked white students to listen to a black student describe how he, as a black man, experienced problems adjusting to college life. The students who were asked to take the black student's perspective by "looking at the world through his eyes and walking through the world in his shoes" expressed more empathy for the specific student and more positive attitudes toward black students in general compared to students who were not asked to take the perspective of the black student. Other studies have shown that perspective-taking increases empathy for and positive attitudes toward a wide variety of groups, including elderly people, individuals who are HIV positive and individuals who speak English as a second language. When we take the time to listen to each other's stories, attempt to take each other's perspective by "looking at the world through his/her eyes and walking through the world in his/her shoes," and travel beyond the boundaries of our culturally homogenous worlds, the gold standard effect will cease.

Focusing on shared characteristics and taking the perspective of the other are small but powerful steps that will lead us toward unity. Together, they can overcome the divisions caused and maintained by categorizing processes gone awry.

Chapter 4 Questions

1. How do your perceptions of other groups affect your interactions with them?

2. We all have a tendency to exaggerate our differences with other cultural groups. Which groups are you more likely to do this with?

3. How do you feel when you are asked to focus on similarities rather than differences?

4. Has someone else ever held you to their cultural group's gold standard? How did you feel?

5. Do you ever find yourself projecting your "gold standard" onto other groups in the church?

6. What would it look like for you to "walk a mile" in an outgroup member's shoes? How would you go about doing that? What, if anything, is preventing you from doing it?

5

Running for Cover

*How the Groups We Form
Protect Our Identity and Self-Esteem*

I recently watched a video podcast in which a nationally known pastor sarcastically denounced a neighboring church's theology. Specifically, he mocked this particular church's overemphasis on a certain aspect of the gospel and underemphasis on another aspect of the gospel. I'm all for lively discourse and I generally agree with the pastor's main point, but I was deeply saddened by the nature and tone of his criticism.

The pastor's analysis of the other church was negative, harsh and distant. It failed to recognize the ways in which the neighboring church was uniquely contributing to the body of Christ and doing some things really well. It was distant in that the pastor criticized from afar, from the safety of his own pulpit rather than engaging in meaningful—although admittedly risky and costly— dialogue with the other church. There is nothing constructive about this form of criticism. In fact, it only serves to make the "correct" pastor and his church members feel better about themselves. Unfortunately, such diatribes are becoming increasingly common within the body of Christ, as group members follow in the divisive footsteps of their pastors and leaders.

Identity and self-esteem—these are powerful forces in our lives. Much like categorizing, they are hidden forces that fuel cultural divisions. We are often unaware of the negative effects of identity and self-esteem on our interactions with other groups. However, while categorizing is primarily a helpful process that unintentionally wreaks havoc on our crosscultural situations, identity and self-esteem processes are driven by a more sinister force: our unmet desire to feel good about ourselves. These processes typically spring up while we are mere schoolchildren. But if left unresolved, they can continue to prevent us from interacting with and finding value in those who are different from us.

The Endless Schoolyard

When I was in high school, I knew a girl we nicknamed Five O'clock Shadow. Perhaps because she was a little awkward and lacked the gleaming weaponry of social status, Five O'clock Shadow didn't belong to any particular friend group. No one wants to be a loner, so she spent most of her free time trailing my group of friends, joining in on our conversations and inviting herself on our group outings.

Five O'clock Shadow simply wanted to fit in—and to her credit, she was a diligent and tenacious tagalong. We made top-secret plans to avoid spending time with her but she always seemed to know where we were headed. If we managed to get away from her for a moment, she would use her uncanny tracking skills and soon discover us. Hence the nickname Five O'clock Shadow—no matter what we did, we simply could not rid ourselves of her.

If we had been mature and compassionate people, and as diligent at being kind as we were at creating witty and cruel nicknames, we would have recognized that she was a genuinely pleasant girl who was toiling for her own social survival and would have welcomed her into the group. But we were high schoolers who were consumed with fighting our own wars of identity and self-esteem. In our shortsightedness, we couldn't think of any good reason to befriend Five O'clock Shadow. She wasn't beautiful according to our narrow definition of beauty. She wasn't a teammate. She wasn't even funny. To sum it up, she didn't add any social currency to our group. If anything, she made our group lose prestige. So we shunned her.

As a volunteer Young Life leader, I witness junior high and high school students vying for acceptance in the same way that Five O'clock Shadow did when I was in school. Being labeled a loser is to be avoided at all costs. The goal is to be identified as someone who is "cool" and, by extension, valuable and good.

Most teenagers will do almost anything to gain significance. This includes banding with others who are similar—those who agree with them, affirm them and confirm that they are in fact valuable and good—and together waging war against other individuals and groups. And lest you think that this sort of behavior is solely caused by adolescent immaturity, it is worth noting that social psychologists have witnessed it in full among adults. The truth is that many of us are still stuck in our high school identity wars. And as we'll come to see clearly, our identity crises are a root cause of the divisions in the body of Christ.

It's no surprise that school kids find themselves engaged in identity wars. Noted developmental psychologist Erik Erikson pointed out that "Who am I?" is a question we begin consciously asking around adolescence and continue asking for the rest of our lives.

We all want to know the answer to the question of identity. Social psychologists believe that the need to know oneself is one of our primary motivations. We hope that what we discover about our identity is good because a positive identity is the route to a positive sense of self. To the extent that we believe that good, valuable and positive things lie within our identity, the better we will feel about ourselves. This is especially important because maintaining high self-esteem is another primary motivation. Not only do we like to know ourselves, we like to believe that we are valuable and good. As T. S. Eliot put it, "Nothing dies harder than the desire to think well of oneself."

Early and influential motivation theorist Abraham Maslow even went so far as to suggest that self-esteem is a basic need that is as important as food and water. There's certainly a lot of evidence to suggest that self-esteem is crucial and well worth fighting for.

First, according to *sociometer theory*, we use self-esteem to determine the extent to which we are accepted or rejected by others in society. In this way, low self-esteem may serve as a warning that we are not well-liked and that perhaps we need to stop being so grumpy or standoffish or whatever it is that we're currently doing and instead seek social support.

Second, *terror management theory* suggests that self-esteem can serve as a buffer against existential anxiety. This idea is based on the fact that most people live with a constant fear of death, although they may not be aware of it. This fear can impair your ability to perform simple, everyday functions that are necessary for survival. If left unchecked, the fear of death can indirectly cause actual death. Fortunately, self-esteem helps to prevent this from happening.

Third, high self-esteem is correlated with positive mental health and helps us to cope with everyday stressors like disappointment, performance pressure, overwhelming emotions and so forth. In sum, self-esteem is quite important and also closely related to identity. So we embark on an exploration of identity, hoping that we will find goodness and value within. But life is complicated and things don't always turn out the way that we hope.

Who am I? The better question might be, *Who do others think I am?* because our self-concept, the part of our self that holds information pertaining to our identity, is extremely susceptible to outside influences. We rely on feedback from other people to gain information about our identity.

On the plus side, others can give us positive information about ourselves that we might not have known otherwise and that can certainly enhance our self-concept. If others treat us as if we're valuable, we're likely to believe that we are valuable. On the negative side, people can also negatively impact our self-concept by telling us that we are unintelligent, unattractive, incapable or worse. Unfortunately, these are the voices that we hear most clearly.

The Negative Speaks Loudest

I have a friend, Mike, who is a well-respected pastor, preacher and leader. One could easily assume that he can write impressive sermons in his sleep. He makes it look that easy. However, Mike recently confessed that every time he sits down to write, he is reminded of the voices of his past that have told him he isn't intelligent and doesn't have anything worthwhile to say. The negative voices of his childhood have the ability to override the many positive ones, if he allows them to. Mike talks of using prayer to "shoo away the demons" before every sermon-writing session. Mike is not the only one who is haunted by negative voices of the past that attempt to override the positive voices and stake claim on our identities.

Given that we live in a fallen world and are surrounded by imperfect people, it is no surprise that many of us embark on our adolescent search for identity by asking "Who am I?" with a dreadful suspicion that we already know the primary answer: not good. John Eldredge and Brent Curtis wrote, "Your evaluation of your soul, which is drawn from a world filled with people still terribly confused about the nature of *their* souls, is probably wrong."

As kids, we often heard voices that were both positive and negative, wanting to believe the positive but haunted by the negative. Thus began our lifelong quest for identity, sometimes car-

rying a chip on our shoulders, wanting to prove that we belong
with all that is good and valuable and not with that which is
lesser and flawed. No wonder so many teenagers are mired in an
identity crisis—they are caught in the crossfire between the positive and negative feedback that comes pouring into their self-
concept. These identity crises can remain unresolved well into
adulthood, however, because group memberships can serve to
harbor our cracked and unstable identities and even create space
for them to thrive.

According to social identity theory, self-esteem is closely tied to
our group memberships because our group identities often overlap
with our sense of self. For example, not only do you think of yourself
as an individual, but you also probably think of yourself in terms of
your many group memberships: gender group, social roles groups
(such as mother, spouse, friend, etc.), ethnic group, occupational
group, church group, even hobby-related groups (book club, fly
fishing, etc.). To the extent that these groups are important to you,
you will expand your sense of self to include them in your identity.

To illustrate this idea, I've created a couple of *highly* scientific
Venn diagrams of Johnny Depp's and Kobe Bryant's identities. Each
circle represents the individual and his group memberships and/or
relationships. As you can see, more important group relationships
take up larger parts of the identity.

The more you are invested in your group memberships, the
more impact they will have on your sense of self and, by extension,
your self-esteem. The relationship between self-esteem and group
membership wouldn't be a big deal except for the fact that whenever
self-esteem is involved, we tend to go on the defensive.

Research on social identity theory has discovered that when it
comes to group membership, we do four things to maintain positive self-esteem: (1) We tend to gravitate toward and form groups
with similar others; (2) once the group is formed we engage in
group-serving biases that defend the group's positive identity; (3)

we try to increase our status by associating with higher-status groups and distancing ourselves from lower-status groups; and (4) if all else fails we literally disparage other groups because in doing so, we elevate our own group.

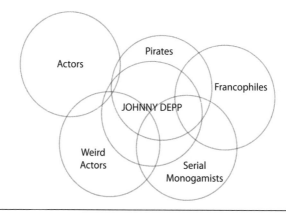

Figure 5.1.

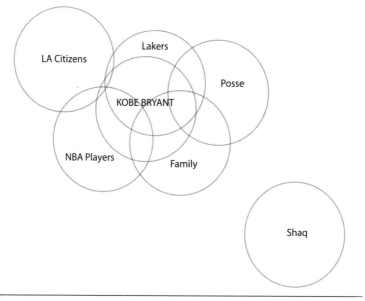

Figure 5.2.

In these ways, our group memberships can help us to fight our identity wars, providing temporary boosts to self-esteem via the group.

Balancing Act

With respect to self-esteem, our group identity is one of our first lines of defense. As such, we tend to choose our groups carefully. Not only do we want to be a member of a high-status group, we also want to surround ourselves with people who will confirm our ideology, thus affirming our own identity and making us feel good about ourselves.

Why do men tend to watch *Braveheart* over and over again in all-male groups while women tend to watch *Pride and Prejudice* again and again in all-female groups? Why don't we watch these movies in mixed company? Because we want to watch with people who generally share our values, will affirm our likes and dislikes, and will grunt/swoon at the appropriate times in the movie.

Few women want to watch *Pride and Prejudice* with a group of men who think that the movie is boring and that Mr. Darcy is anything less than perfect. Likewise, few men want to watch *Braveheart* with a group of women who don't get inspired by that stupid speech that Mel Gibson/William Wallace gives right before they all die. And so it goes.

We tend to stick with people who like what we like—those who talk, eat, interact, believe and perceive the world like us. John Stott intuitively stated that, "The people we immediately, instinctively like, and find it easy to get on with are the people who give us the respect we consider we deserve. . . . In other words, personal vanity is a key factor in all our relationships."

A more cognitive explanation for our desire to form allegiances with similar others is found in Fritz Heider's *balance theory*. According to this theory, humans are motivated to maintain cognitive "balance" within relationships with others. In other words, we are comfortable when we agree with others on important issues, and we experience a palpable cognitive discomfort when we don't agree. As such, we tend to pursue and maintain relationships with people with whom we can agree—with whom we have achieved "balance." Heider developed a balance triangle to illustrate his theory.

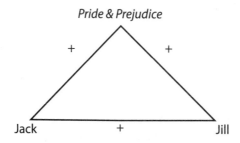

Pride & Prejudice

Jack + Jill

Example of a balanced relationship.
Jill loves *P & P.* Jack does too. (Clearly, Jack is perfect.)
They continue to grow closer.

Figure 5.3.

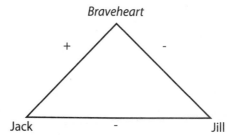

Braveheart

Jack - Jill

Example of an unbalanced relationship.
Jill thinks *Braveheart* is pointless. Jack says it's epic, *simply EPIC.*
Jack and Jill are unable to maintain a close relationship.

Figure 5.4.

Within the context of crosscultural situations in the body of Christ, our need for affirmation creates a greater desire to surround ourselves with those who subscribe to our culturally distinct ways of life and an aversion to those whose mere difference threatens our unstable identities. We want to be affirmed. So we intentionally seek out the best people from whom to receive affirmation: those who share our values and priorities.

Our self-image and identity are at stake here. Groups that affirm who we are can help us to defend the assaults we are already dealing with. In this sense, groups can serve as havens for our afflicted selves, and for a few fleeting moments, we feel better about ourselves.

Social Climbing

If your current group is not patting you on the back enough and making you feel good about yourself, you still have an option. You can simply leave the group and try to gain membership in a better one. Since group membership largely informs self-esteem, it makes sense that humans are motivated to join groups that meet their self-esteem needs. This often means joining a high-status group.

Robert Cialdini has conducted research that shows that people "bask in reflected glory" (BIRG) by associating with high-status people. In one study, Cialdini found that individuals felt better about themselves if they knew that a stranger who was superficially connected to them (such as with a shared birth date) had performed well on an intelligence test. By simply associating with a high-status person or group, people felt better about themselves, even when the reason for the association was quite trivial. (This helps to explain why, when people ask me how to spell my last name, I smugly offer, "Cleveland, like the president.")

In another study, Cialdini and his colleagues wanted to see if BIRGing extends to group memberships. They decided to test whether college students were more likely to associate with their respective school when it had recently experienced success—in other words, when it was riding a wave of high status.

During football season one year, the researchers monitored students on the Mondays after football games on the campuses of Arizona State University, Purdue University, Notre Dame University and Ohio State University and recorded whether students were wearing clothes with their school's name on it. They found that students wore more school-identifying clothing after a team victory than after a team defeat! They also found that students were more likely to say, "*We* won!" when their school's team had been successful and "*They* lost!" when their school's team had been unsuccessful. So people BIRG by associating with winners.

Dumping Your Group

There's an overwhelming amount of BIRGing going on in the body of Christ. In our own quests for significance, we often identify with the Christians who are valued in our communities. We tend to gravitate toward churches that "look good"—from presentation to population to property—because to be associated with an organization that is successful and attractive makes us look like we are successful and attractive. Only hipsters attend the hip church. Therefore if I attend, I must be hip. Only intellectuals attend the intellectual church. Therefore if I attend, I must be intellectual. Only true reconcilers attend the multiethnic church. Therefore if I attend, I must be a true reconciler. Years after high school graduation, we're still looking for significance.

Another social identity theorist named C. R. Snyder observed that in addition to increasing self-esteem by BIRGing, people also reliably boost and maintain self-esteem by distancing themselves from losers. Snyder coined the term "cutting off reflected failure" (CORFing) to describe this tendency.

In one important study, Snyder and his colleagues told participants that they would be working in teams on a problem-solving project under time pressure. Participants were also told that once they completed their project, they would be making a presentation on their project findings in front of a panel of judges and members of other teams. Once the groups completed the task, an experimenter pretended to evaluate their performance and, in doing so, led them to believe that they had either performed very well or very poorly. (The feedback that the teams received was randomly predetermined, so it didn't have anything to do with their actual performance.)

The researchers then measured the extent to which participants CORFed in two ways. First, they asked participants if they would prefer to opt out of giving the presentation. They found that participants who had been placed on low-performing teams had very little interest in being publicly associated with their team. However, participants on the high-performing teams couldn't wait to stand in front of a group of people and talk about how amazing they were.

Second, the researchers gave participants the opportunity to pick up and wear a badge identifying them with their team. Predictably, team members on low-performing teams CORFed, choosing not to wear a badge that identified them with their loser teammates, and high-performing team members strutted out of the lab adorned with their team badges.

Snyder's study was the first to show that both BIRGing and CORFing play a significant role in helping group members to attain and maintain high self-esteem. The participants didn't think twice about ditching their groups in favor of preserving their self-esteem. It also showed that often our self-esteem takes priority over group memberships. We tend to remain in the group as long as it's good for our self-esteem. But if the going gets tough and our self-esteem starts to suffer, we're likely to change group membership in order to preserve our self-esteem.

Of course, this is mostly the case for those groups that have fluid group memberships. For some groups, membership is more or less permanent—such as ethnic groups, socioeconomic groups and groups based on ability. What if it isn't feasible to ditch your group? In other words, what if you're stuck with a low-status group for a long period of time or even indefinitely? How do you CORF (and maintain self-esteem) when you can't easily walk away?

Some of my own research begins to answer this question. By

relying on deception and confederates (members of my research team who pose as real participants in the experiment), I create elaborate, simulated social worlds in which I examine group processes, including group identity.

In a recent five-week-long experiment, we examined the behavior of eighty-five teams, each composed of one real participant and two confederates. Of course, the participants had no idea that their teammates were in on the ruse. By placing the teams in a relatively long-term situation, I was able to observe the tactics that participants use to preserve self-esteem when physically distancing themselves from the team is not an option.

In the experiment, teams competed in an anagram tournament in which they needed to unscramble strings of letters to form words. The participants were led to believe that they were competing against real teams filled with other people who were participating in the experiment. In addition, we rigged the tournament so that half of the teams in the experiment won all of their anagram contests (high-status condition) and half of them lost all of their contests (low-status condition). In this way, we were able to compare the high-status teams and low-status teams. We also rigged it so that half of the participants were the best performers on their team and the other half were the worst performers on the team. In order to do this, the confederates memorized all of the solutions to the anagrams beforehand, so that they could easily outperform or underperform the participant as needed.

Basically we created a scenario in which at least some of the participants in the study (that is, the ones on the low-status teams) would be motivated to CORF. No one wants to be in a low-status group, especially when you're the best performer on the team. But the low-status group members in this experiment were unable to walk away or attempt to join a higher-status group, mainly because they were committed to completing the study. So what did they do?

We asked participants whether they would leave their team and join a better team if given the opportunity. On average, participants on high-status teams said no, which makes sense because when the going is good, we tend to sit back and accept the status quo. But participants on low-status teams said yes. Interestingly, the participants who were the best performers on low-status teams were the most interested in joining a higher-status team. If we perceive that we are better than our fellow group members, we're more likely to want to upgrade to a higher-status group.

It should be noted that participants on high-status teams showed signs of BIRGing behavior. They didn't just *talk* of strongly identifying with their teammates, liking them and wanting to spend time with them; they walked the walk too. The confederates on high-status teams reported that the participants on their teams often invited them to parties, to coffee and other social gatherings both while they were participating in the study and long after the study officially ended. The participants often shared private information about their lives, relationships and so forth with the confederates. And participants on high-status teams often asked the confederates to be their friends on Facebook (a sign of authentic friendship, if there ever was one). Being on a high-status team was good for their self-esteem, so participants connected with the group in numerous ways both inside and outside of the lab. In short, participants on high-status teams showed classic signs of BIRGing.

However, we were most interested in whether participants on low-status teams discovered ways to CORF when simply walking away wasn't a plausible option. How did they save face by setting themselves apart from their low-status teammates? One, they began to identify less and less with the group. They couldn't quit the group, so they just began to care less and less about it over time. By the end of the study, the participants in the low-status group reported significantly lower identification with the team than participants in the high-status group. This makes sense in light of the fact that self-esteem is highly connected to identity. As such, the

best way to prevent losses in self-esteem is to become less identified with the low-status group. If you can't physically walk away,
you can certainly emotionally walk away.

Additionally, participants on low-status teams were less affected
by their teammates' poor performance; they felt less obligated to
help their struggling teammates because they hardly identified
with their teammates. Participants on low-status teams also reported less of a desire to spend time with their teammates in social
settings outside of the lab. They knew that they were required to
interact with the group while they were in the lab, but they didn't
want to be caught dead with their low-status teammates out in the
real world.

Participants on low-status teams did not like or care about their
teammates as much as participants on high-status teams. The participants on low-status teams used less common CORFing tactics,
but the effect was the same. Relative to participants on high-status
teams, participants on low-status teams didn't identify with their
teammates, like their teammates or want to spend time with their
teammates. They were teammates in name but not in heart. This was
good for self-esteem preservation, but not so good for team unity.

Sometimes we followers of Christ are like the high-performing
participants on the low-status teams in my experiment. We can't
literally walk away from the "teammates in Christ" that we don't
like or value. So we do the next best thing: we start to identify less
and less with them. We stop caring about their needs and struggles.
And we stop spending so much time with them in public. Ultimately, we decrease our identification with the church full of the
low-status ethnic group, or the not-so-trendy church that is still
living in the twentieth (maybe the nineteenth) century, or the
socioeconomically disadvantaged church, or the rigid fundamentalist church, or the super liberal church that is sliding uncontrol-
lably down the slippery slope, because to identify with them would
make us look bad. We accomplish this by exaggerating our differ-

ences with culturally different Christians (as I described in chapter 4) and by clinging to our subordinate identities (e.g., identities based on ethnic, denominational, theological or political affiliations) while distancing ourselves from our common identity—our identity as members of the worldwide body of Christ. It's more important for us to feel good ourselves than to embrace other members of the body of Christ. This is how we compensate.

In the end, we may technically share group membership and the label of "followers of Christ," but we are no longer a team. We are driven by our own needs, not the needs of the entire group. We are teammates in name but not in heart. Our ability to unite with the entire body of Christ is seriously impeded when our primary concern is to preserve our self-esteem.

It's Like Being Married

My parents, who are experts on marriage, talk a lot about how a healthy marriage is all about sticking together for richer and for poorer, for better and for worse and in sickness and in health. (Apparently, the person who wrote the traditional wedding vows was on to something.) As my mom would put it, sometimes my dad smells fresh and clean, other times he really doesn't. Sometimes his heart is in the right place, other times it's not. Sometimes he's easy to get along with, other times he's less so. Sometimes he makes my mom proud, other times his words or actions embarrass her or cause her pain. (And vice versa, of course.)

But no matter what, for thirty-four good years and counting, my parents have stuck together through thick and thin. Their identities are irrevocably intertwined. So even when they don't see eye to eye on an important issue, when one has disappointed the other or when it seems like it would make the most sense to quit and go their separate ways, they stay. They keep talking. They keep praying for each other. They keep loving each other. They stay close to each other. Quite simply, CORFing is *not* an option, even if it might temporarily boost their self-esteem. Their submission to God, binding commitment to each other and interdependence drive their interactions with each other, and their need to feel good about themselves does not come at the expense of commitment to the other.

Remember the Venn diagrams I used to describe Kobe Bryant's and Johnny Depp's identities? I created one to illustrate my parents' awesome marriage.

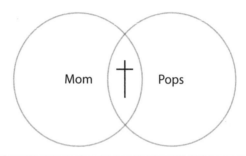

Figure 5.5.

I think that this picture of healthy marriage is a great model for how the body of Christ should work. Theoretically, married people can't quit a marriage. In the same way, theoretically, Christians can't quit the body of Christ. Our commitment to the other members of the body of Christ should trump our desire to CORF when the going gets tough and it would be better for our self-esteem if we just walked away—like when we disagree on an important issue, or when the other group's heart isn't in the right place and they hurt us, or when the other group speaks a different language. Our submission to God, irrevocable commitment to each other and interdependence should hold us together when we want to distance ourselves from Christians who fail to live up to our gold standards or who complicate our lives.

Unfortunately, for the most part, our divided body of Christ is not living up to this ideal. Our identities tend not to overlap across

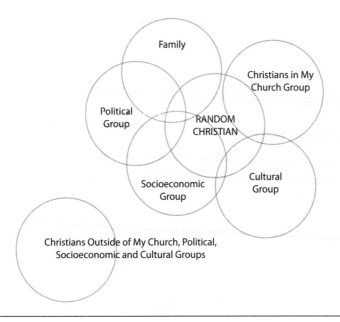

Figure 5.6.

cultural lines, and our commitment to Christ is not holding us together. Instead, our need to feel good about ourselves often comes at the expense of commitment to each other.

This is disconcerting. The body of Christ is like a bad marriage.

What Now?

I recently watched a movie called *Music Within*, a biopic about Richard Pimentel, the man who spent years fighting on behalf of differently abled Americans and is largely responsible for the Americans with Disabilities Act (ADA). It's hard for most people to believe that the ADA-compliant buildings, elevators, ramps, restrooms and so on that many of us take for granted were merely a pipedream before Pimentel decided to fight for their existence.

Early on, Pimentel faced a fierce, uphill battle. He quickly realized that the American public just didn't care about differently abled people; few people were willing to spend money training differently abled employees or remodeling their buildings to make them handicap accessible. The American people had essentially CORFed; they weren't connected to or invested in the lives of the differently abled.

One day, after receiving yet another indifferent response from a potential employer, Pimentel expressed his frustration to one of his differently abled friends, wondering aloud how he could change the way the American public perceived differently abled people. His friend's response was incredibly insightful. He said, "You don't need to change how they see [differently abled] people. You need to change how they see themselves."

You see, Americans had developed an identity that did not include differently abled people; differently abled people were outgroup members. So when they were asked to go out of their way to care for a differently abled person, they were unwilling or unable to do so. Quite simply, the identities of the differently abled and the rest of the American public were *not* irrevocably intertwined—their respective Venn diagrams weren't even on the same page! Pimentel quickly realized that the best way to get Americans to care about the differently abled was to convince Americans to expand their identities to reach out and include the differently abled. He needed to convince Americans that *to be American* meant to care about other Americans, including the differently abled. He changed the way Americans saw themselves, and in doing so, he changed the way Americans saw differently abled people.

This approach will work for the body of Christ too. We need to adopt the belief that *to be a follower of Christ* means to care deeply about and pursue other followers of Christ, including the ones that we don't instinctively value or like. We need to adopt the belief that to be a follower of Christ means to allow our identity as members of the body of Christ to trump all other identities. We need to adopt the belief that to be a follower of Christ means to put our commitment to the body of Christ above our own identity and self-esteem needs. We've coped with our divisions long enough. It's time for us to discover our true identities as members of the family of God. It's time for us to rally around this identity, overcome our divisions and change the world. In sum, it's time for us to change the way we see ourselves.

Redefining What It Means to Be "Us"

This sort of reorientation is an intimidating task because we tend to think of identity as somewhat permanent. We talk about identity being "rooted" in things. In addition, we're only given permission to have identity crises twice during our long lifetimes: during adolescence and middle age. But the truth is that identity is constantly morphing, depending on the situation.

Research has shown that our awareness of our identity is often determined by those who are around us. This happens most when we are engaged in tasks or social situations that remind us that we identify with a particular group or role, and as a result we become consciously aware of this identity.

I am an Oakland A's baseball fan. Billy Beane is my hero; I grew up cheering on the Bash Brothers in the '80s; and later when I was in college, I had an idolatrous crush on pitcher Barry Zito. It's safe to say that I am a true A's fan and that I always possess the identity of an A's fan. However, my identity as an A's fan is not always at the forefront of my conscious mind. (Social psychologists would say it is not always *salient*.) It does not always influence the way that I interact with the world. Rather, this only happens under certain circumstances, such as when I see a fellow A's fan on the street or when I'm watching the A's play. It happens when I spend money on tickets, bond with other fans (people about whom I would otherwise care very little) and take time out of my busy day to watch lengthy games. My identity as an A's fan isn't at the forefront of my consciousness the rest of the time—it comes and goes depending on the situation.

One of my friends recently returned from a large, international Christian conference in South Africa. At the conference, he listened to numerous talks given in native tongues and translated into dozens of languages. He also spent time worshiping God in many different languages and cultural styles. As a result of that situational experience, he returned to the United States with a strong sense of his identity as a member of the worldwide body of Christ. Consequently, his identity as a Minnesota Methodist became less important than his identity as a member of the worldwide body of Christ. His identity as a member of the body of Christ was prominently situated at the forefront of his consciousness, whereas his identity as a Minnesota Methodist was pushed to the background.

Depending on what we're thinking about and whom we've surrounded ourselves with, our different identities will toggle back and forth between the forefront and background of our consciousness. When a certain identity is in the forefront of our mind, that identity will immediately impact our sense of self. This is important because identity determines how we process information in social situations and how we respond to others. Researchers who study close relationships have found that our identity often expands to include others who are physically and emotionally close to us. When this happens, simply thinking about ourselves automatically triggers thoughts of the other people who overlap with our identities. At this point, they are a part of "us," our family—we couldn't distance ourselves from them even if we tried! Further, our interests and investments begin to overlap with theirs. What breaks their heart begins to break our heart too. What makes them smile begins to make us smile too. Our actions toward them are perceived as actions toward us. To care about them is to care about us. To treat them well is to treat us well. In this process, they go from outgroup members to ingroup members and so we begin to treat them like ingroup members. We typically like our ingroup members, so it's no surprise that we ultimately find ourselves liking them too.

Noted groups researcher John Turner once said that "the attractiveness of an individual is not constant, but varies with group membership." We like people with whom we identify and whom we consider to be a part of our ingroup. If we diversify our friend groups (more later on *how* this should be done) and start to invest in friendships across cultural lines, our identity will expand to include those culturally different groups. To the extent that culturally different members of the body of Christ are included in our identity and ingroup, we'll resist the urge to ditch them when the going gets tough or in order to save our self-esteem. This idea gives me hope that members of the body of Christ can experience significant and much-needed identity shifts that will bring us closer toward unity.

But before we can address this problem head-on, we must think a bit more about how identity and self-esteem affect our interactions with each other.

Chapter 5 Questions

1. Think back to your earlier days as a junior high kid. Can you recall feeling the urge to BIRG (bask in reflected glory) or CORF (cut off reflected failure) in order to maintain self-esteem?

2. How do you think your desire to feel good about yourself as a kid affected your perceptions of and interactions with others?

3. How do you see yourself and/or other Christians BIRGing today? What do you think causes you to do it? How does BIRGing affect your identity and self-esteem?

4. How do you see yourself and/or other Christians CORFing today? What do you think causes you to do it? How does CORFing affect your identity and self-esteem?

5. How do you think the CORFing that you and/or other Christians do affects outgroup members (i.e., the people who are cut off)?

6. What strategies might you use to stop BIRGing and CORFing in the body of Christ?

6

Waging Identity Wars

How Bias Boosts Our Self-Esteem

B*ack in 1951 when Ivy League football* was still relevant, Dartmouth and Princeton played an important game. The game was an unbelievably rough one. By the end of the third quarter, a Princeton player's nose had been broken and a Dartmouth player's leg had been broken, and both teams had received multiple penalties for foul play.

Researchers at Dartmouth and Princeton took advantage of this opportunity to measure Dartmouth and Princeton fans' perceptions of the game. They discovered that both groups believed that their respective team was less responsible for the foul play than the rival team. "*They're* the problem! *They're* playing like thugs. *We're* just the victims!" each group proclaimed. Even though both teams had received numerous penalties for foul play, neither group of fans was willing to admit that their team had contributed to the problem. Even the schools' newspapers were biased in their reports!

Not only do we use our group to create affirming spaces for our beleaguered identities, but we also shore up self-esteem by perceiving situations in biased ways. We want to believe that we, and by extension our groups, are good and valuable, so we go to great and even irrational lengths to maintain positive perceptions of ourselves. And we often do it without being aware that we are doing it. Since we desperately need self-esteem, our minds have built-in self-serving biases that protect it. These biases help us to naturally interpret the world in ways that make ourselves look good. By doing so, we preserve our sense of self and maintain positive self-esteem.

One way we engage in self-serving biases is by choosing to participate in situations and tasks in which we can shine. There's a reason why people who are good at solving math problems but terrible at solving interpersonal problems become engineers rather than human resources managers.

A second practice is to make self-serving attributions. For example, we often overestimate our personal contributions to successful projects and underestimate our contributions to unsuccessful projects. If a team project goes well, we tend to think that it's due to our personal efforts, savvy and expertise. If a team project goes poorly, we blame it on someone else.

A third way we employ self-serving biases is by choosing to compare ourselves to lower-status people rather than higher-status people. The B student will likely compare himself to a C student rather than an A student because compared to the C student, the B student looks like a relative genius.

Do these self-serving biases actually work? Well, North Americans tend to feel pretty good about themselves. The fact that the average North American claims to have above-average self-esteem suggests that these self-serving biases are doing their job.

Sometimes self-serving biases work a little *too* well, however. Almost everyone rates themselves as better than average on a variety of traits and abilities including fairness, virtuosity, ability to get along with others and investment savvy. Obviously, it isn't statistically possible for *everyone* to be better than average on these traits and abilities. We all believe that we are better than average, but the truth is that some of us are sadly mistaken. (But not you or me, of course.)

Defending Your Group

Since our self-esteem is so closely tied to group membership (see chapter 5), we tend to go on the defensive when it comes to protecting our group identity just like we go on the defensive when it comes to protecting our individual identity. Not surprisingly, we engage in all of the same self-serving biases but we apply them to our groups. We tend to participate in activities that will enhance our group's image, overestimate our group's contribution to successful efforts and compare ourselves to lower-status groups. And much like the mid-twentieth century Dartmouth and Princeton football fans, we will even go to great lengths to interpret ambiguous situations in ways that make us look good and make the other group look awful.

Many local communities have an annual interchurch worship service or prayer meeting, typically around the National Day of Prayer. If these events are somewhat successful, group-serving biases are likely to lead us to believe that our church was critical to the success. "Yeah, the speaker from the Latino church was pretty good, but it was really our church's worship band that got the night going," we whisper to ourselves. However, if the event goes poorly, we blame everyone else, even God. The only thing we know for sure is that it's not *our* fault. In the end, we concede that unity just isn't meant to be, and we retreat back to our separate groups, divisions and self-esteem still intact.

Even if our group possesses negative characteristics or experiences failure, we can use group-serving biases to perceive a better picture of our group and continue to feel good about our group identity.

The problem is that when we rely on group-serving biases to maintain our positive group identity, we tend to adopt a defensive and unreconciliatory stance. Regardless of the situation, in our eyes, our particular group is superior. By thinking highly of ourselves, we naturally think less of others. There might be social problems in the world, but *our* group is not responsible for them. That other group is the cause of all of the ills. There might be friction within our local community of Christians, but *we're* innocent. The problem would be solved if the other church would vote differently, or get serious about living the Christian life, or get their theology straight. They need us, but since we're perfect, we don't need them.

These biases can prevent us from receiving useful insight from those outside our group. In chapter 3, we talked about the ways in which categorizing makes it difficult for us to receive useful information from outgroup members. Social identity processes amplify the problem. If someone critiques our group's theology or lifestyle or political ideology, we are unable to receive it because we're too busy protecting our positive group identity. Essentially, our defensiveness disables our ability to humbly receive correction and instruction.

Sticks and Stones

I know that this is a tad bit dark, but if someone approached me, confessing an uncomfortable bout of low self-esteem and asking for a quick and dirty boost to their self-esteem, I would advise that person to put someone else down. The unfortunate truth is that the easiest and most effective way to boost your own image is to lower someone else's.

Most of us learn this the moment we step foot on an elementary school playground. By the time we reach high school, we are quite skilled at both blatant and subtle putdowns. Two social psychologists, Steven Fein and Steven Spencer, have collected data that suggest that this is a well-learned skill that even adults use when necessary. Fein and Spencer believe that prejudice and negative evaluations often come from our need to maintain high feelings of self-worth. The more we feel that our self-image is threatened, the more likely we will put others down in order to regain a positive self-image.

In one important study, they tested this idea in two steps. First, they tested whether people who were in need of a self-esteem boost would be more likely to disparage someone outside their group. Second, they tested whether the act of disparaging someone actually boosted self-esteem.

In the experiment, they asked non-Jewish participants to complete an intelligence test. Upon completion of the test, participants received bogus feedback on their scores. Half of the participants in the study were told that they had performed very well (the 93rd percentile), and the other half were told that . . . well, that they're not exactly the brightest crayon in the box. The idea was that the people who received negative feedback would be looking for an opportunity to boost their self-esteem.

After receiving the bogus feedback, participants were asked to evaluate the personality of either an ingroup member (a non-Jewish, European American woman) or an outgroup member (a Jewish woman). Then each participant's self-esteem was measured.

Fein and Spencer found that participants who had received positive feedback on their intelligence test evaluated both the European American (ingroup member) and Jewish (outgroup member) women equally highly. They felt good about themselves, so they didn't need to put anyone else down. However, participants whose self-image was threatened by the negative feedback on the intelligence test rated the European American woman (ingroup member) positively but the Jewish woman (outgroup member) negatively. (Believe it or not, this study was conducted in 1997, not 1927!)

By evaluating the Jewish woman negatively, participants were able to recover the self-esteem that they lost when they found out they were less than smart. When our self-esteem is high and intact, we are not likely to put outsiders down. But when we're suffering an identity crisis, we take cheap shots at other groups in order to feel better about ourselves.

It's worth pointing out that the participants in the study didn't need to torch a Jewish temple or bully the Jewish woman into eating nonkosher food in order to feel better about themselves. They didn't need to take drastic and dramatic physical measures. They simply needed to say, "Her personality is not that great" or "She's kind of lame" or "She's not very cool" and their self-esteem was immediately restored.

This is the sort of subtle belittling that runs rampant on elementary school playgrounds, in high school hallways and within the body of Christ. We don't often picket each other's churches or boycott each other's events, but we do often make snarky comments that threaten our unity in subtle but potent ways. Rather than reaching out to contribute to what God is doing in other church groups, we'd prefer to sit back and talk about how they're missing the point or going about it all wrong.

Doing this widens the divide between followers of Christ. We do it because our allegiances are with our particular church group (and not with the larger body of Christ) and because we use our group identity to maintain a positive sense of self.

Research conducted by Fein and Spencer and others suggests that those who derogate other groups are doing so at least partly because their identity is threatened. According to this research, the very presence of divisions in the body of Christ indicates that too many of us are still fighting the identity wars of our adolescence and that we are relying on the same tried and true tactics.

This could be due to the fact that at the start of our quest for identity, many of us bought into the idea that our primary identity should be found in groups with like-minded others. Examples of these types of groups are ethnic groups, socioeconomic groups, political groups, groups based on popularity or attractiveness, and denominations. We joined these groups (or similar ones) when we were in high school and they continue to inform our identity today.

In many cases, these are the groups that we rely on to maintain our positive identity, in which we are highly invested and care very much about. When we need a self-esteem boost, we use our cultural group memberships to wage war, defending our groups and increasing their status by any means necessary—just like we did when we were in high school. Unfortunately, this occurs at the expense of other groups' dignity.

Group memberships based on ethnicity, political affiliation and so forth are not bad per se. In fact, they can be quite useful. The problem is that, if we place too much value in them, they can prevent us from finding our identity in grander, far more important groups. In this case, the grander, far more important group that often gets overlooked is the body of Christ.

In our quests for identity, we seem to have drifted off course, gaining identity and esteem from less meaningful groups rather than forging on toward our truest identity as members of the body of Christ. In addition to dealing with lingering identity issues from childhood, many Christians today are also experiencing an identity crisis due to societal changes.

Over the last century, Western moral standards have drifted further away from traditional Christian and biblical standards, Christians are often portrayed as bigoted or dumb in the media, and public education has become increasingly secularized. As a result, many Christians have adopted a defensive stance toward those who pose a threat to their identities, both Christian and otherwise.

The factors that lead culturally threatened Christians to lash out at others will be discussed in greater detail in chapter 7. For now, let's just stop to consider how we ourselves wage identity wars with other groups in the body of Christ.

I know that as an unmarried, urban, professional woman of color, I have used my mosaic of identities to wage war against other women in the body of Christ. This didn't happen intentionally but it happened all the same. By the time I reached my late twenties, I'd lost touch with my friends who married young and became stay-at-home suburban moms to multiple children. Our life paths diverged when I discovered that maintaining a friendship with women with vastly different schedules, locations, responsibilities and perspectives required Olympian-level logistical gymnastics and was no easy feat.

As a result, I naturally fell into a social and spiritual world that was almost devoid of meaningful interactions with stay-at-home moms. Predictably (see chapter 3), the simple segregation resulted in inaccurate perceptions that robbed me of a desire to form rich friendships with this group of women. However, my lack of desire for friendships with stay-at-home moms was spurred on by my own identity and self-esteem issues—namely, my difficulties in carving a path for myself in the Christian world. I often observed that the Christian world validated more traditional female roles, and my identity was threatened by what I perceived to be a lack of support for my nontraditional path. For this reason, I incorrectly identified stay-at-home moms (who in my mind embodied the narrow Christian female ideal that threatened my worldview and way of life) as willful contributors to my misery. Consequently, I had no problem avoiding them and even devaluing them. Rather than addressing my deep need to feel good about myself in a healthy way, I boosted my self-esteem by launching prejudicial grenades at other women.

Upon realizing my own contribution to this particular division in the body of Christ, I repented of my prejudice and joined a weekly "mom Bible study" at my church, at which I opined little and listened much. Over time, I discovered that many stay-at-home moms actually felt threatened by the likes of me and that we had mutually labeled each other the enemy while losing sight of the fact that we have a very real, very cunning Enemy who works relentlessly to get us to devalue and antagonize each other. I was also reminded that I don't know everything and that stay-at-home moms have a perspective that I desperately need.

The potent combination of spending most of my time with women who were just like me and using my group memberships to bolster my own beleaguered identity resulted in a seemingly impenetrable division that prevented me from seeking to understand and form bonds with my diverse sisters.

If we honestly examine the ways that our self-esteem and identity affect our interactions with other cultural groups, we'll probably discover that we engage in identity wars much like the one that I described above. In addition, we often claim most of the credit for successful efforts. We tend to shift the blame for societal ills to other groups. We tend to care more about our fellow church group members than members of other Christian groups. We often distance ourselves from church groups that are composed of individuals who are not highly valued by society or are negatively affecting our group's PR. We often ridicule, undermine and put down other groups. We are often stingy when it comes to praising other church groups, especially those that are fundamentally different from our group. And most importantly, we are separate.

Our separation is tantamount because it indicates that we still have not settled on our true identity. When we apply research on social identity theory to the body of Christ, we have to conclude that if there is anything preventing us from uniting with other followers of Jesus who look, think, act, speak, vote, smell differently, then it's likely that we need to clarify our identity as members of the body of Christ.

What Now?

We must find our true source of self-esteem, restore our true identity and relativize all others if we're going to have a fighting chance at unity. I believe that the metaphor of the body of Christ, which preaches mutual crosscultural interdependence, was designed to rescue us from homogeneity and remind us of our truest identity—as diverse people united in Christ. However, one challenge is that we aren't consciously aware of how our cultural group memberships overpower our common identity as members of the body of Christ. We must do the difficult work of examining our hearts and reflecting on our attitudes toward other groups in order to uncover, uproot and repent of the deep biases that self-esteem and identity processes have ingrained in us. Then we must affirm our truest, common identities as members of the body of Christ.

Who Me? Biased?

There are a large number of influential pastors in the Twin Cities metropolitan area. Pastors with thousands and thousands of Twitter followers, adored in some Christian circles and disdained in others, armed with legions of fanboys who defend their theological views to the point of death, and even with a few bona fide death-threat-spewing enemies. For better or for worse, they are the Pauls and Apolloses of our era.

For the past few months, I've been teaching a class on intercultural ministry leadership at a local seminary. Depending on their theological tradition, the students in my class have very strong opinions in favor of or against each of the well-known pastors in our area. So in the middle of an exercise on valuing culturally different viewpoints, I asked my students to watch a short video of one of these pastors discussing practical theology and to make a list of all of the things that they can learn from this pastor. I know that *hate* is a strong word, but I think it's safe to say that most of the students in my class hate this particular pastor—or at the very least, they hate a lot of what he stands for. So I wasn't at all surprised when my students refused to admit that they could learn anything from him. In fact, several of my students gave me the stink eye for even showing the video in the first place! One possible sign that you have succumbed to self-esteem and identity-fueled divisions is that you're unwilling to admit that *they* have something valuable to teach you.

Here are some other signs that you may have succumbed to self-esteem and identity-related divisions:

- You cringe at the thought of praising a particular Christian group.

- When someone tries to associate you with a particular group, you overreact and go out of your way to clarify that you are not with *them*.

- You don't even want to be exposed to the ideas or ways of a particular group, much less earnestly listen to them.

- You can't bring yourself to admit that you are in fact threatened by another group's success, prominence or influence.

The Sermon Didn't Kill Me

Once we have identified and repented of our self-esteem and identity-related divisions, we must do the hard work of overcoming them. I believe that *self-affirmation theory* can help. We already know that when our self-image is threatened, we go on the defensive and do whatever it takes to feel good about ourselves. This often includes derogating different groups. Well, research on self-affirmation theory has found that derogating other groups isn't the only effective way to regain self-esteem. Another powerful way to regain self-esteem is to simply affirm the self, even if you affirm a part of the self that is unrelated to the part that has been threatened. When people affirm another aspect of their self—by, say, writing an essay about an important value that they hold—they are more secure in their self-worth and less defensive when their identity is threatened.

I actually practiced self-affirmation this morning. One of my friends asked me to listen to a sermon that his well-known pastor recently preached on the roles of women in the family and church. This topic makes my blood boil, and I generally find this pastor's beliefs and communication style to be oppressive to women. But I believe that it's important to earnestly listen to diverse viewpoints, even on issues that are central to my self-esteem and identity. Call me crazy, but I think of it as a spiritual discipline of sorts. So I told my friend that I'd watch a video podcast of the sermon.

I knew that if I affirmed my identity as a member of the body of Christ, affirmed my belief that Christ is the head of the body (and not me or anyone else) and affirmed the truth that all others in the body of Christ are connected to me, I would be better able to listen humbly without thinking that I know everything there is to know about gender and Christianity and without desperately needing to boost my self-esteem by derogating Famous Pastor. Because, let's be honest: it would be useless to watch the sermon with a defensive identity that was entirely rooted in being right about the issue of women in the church and Famous Pastor's idiocy. I also knew that an identity firmly rooted in the body of Christ would serve to buffer any pain that watching the sermon might cause.

For many historically oppressed people in the church (e.g., women, people of color, etc.), crosscultural journeys with the goal of connecting to the other parts of the body come at great cost and great risk. All of the parts of the body are composed of sinful human beings who often fail at loving other parts of the body well. But due to inequitable power structures in the body of Christ, certain demographic groups have more power and influence with which they can do great good or cause great pain. Sometimes (and perhaps this is unintentional), empowered individuals or groups in the church inflict excruciating pain onto disempowered individuals or groups. By listening to this pastor's sermon, I was potentially exposing myself to a hurtful idea communicated in a condescending way that could inflict pain upon me and, in doing so, dishonor the *imago Dei* in me. Despite this possibility, I believe that

I am called to remain connected to the body of Christ, even if that means enduring such pain. But I don't have to do it without protection. Affirming my identity as a member of the body of Christ and as a bearer of the *imago Dei* could effectively buffer me from pain. (We'll address this tricky and serious issue of power in the church in greater detail in chapter 9. Get ready!)

So I did some self-affirmation exercises. As you've probably guessed, self-affirmation for followers of Christ is basically just a focused "quiet time." Before listening to the sermon, I read, prayed through and meditated on passages in the Bible that affirmed my identity as a member of the body of Christ and affirmed my identity as a woman who bears God's image. These passages reminded me that my identity and significance are not based on my ministry ability or what I believe or whether well-known pastors affirm my beliefs or preach hurtful ideas about me. They reminded me that my identity and significance are rooted in my membership in the family of God. My beliefs and calling are important, but they aren't the most defining things about me.

The passages I read during the self-affirmation exercises reminded me that this famous pastor whose sermon I was about to watch was not just some guy who spouts ideas that are hurtful to me. As a fellow member of the family of God, he's irrevocably connected to me; I can't just dismiss him as one of *them*. Like the hand needs the nose, I need him and he needs me. As such, my posture toward him should be gracious and inviting, actively looking for ways to display the mutual interdependence that the body of Christ is all about, regardless of whether he ever reciprocates or is deemed worthy of relationship with me in my own eyes. Of equal importance, my time of reflection on the body of Christ reminded me that Christ, not this particular pastor, is the head of the family. I don't have to fear what this pastor might say because ultimately, he's not God. What a relief.

I spent about twenty-five minutes doing the self-affirmation exercises and then watched the forty-five-minute sermon while working out on my elliptical machine. The fact that I'm writing about this right now is proof that the self-affirmation exercises worked; the sermon didn't kill me! But in all seriousness, when my identity is rooted in the right place, I'm able to listen to opposing viewpoints as a member of the body of Christ: with humility, with an eagerness to learn from a different point of view, with a desire to connect across cultural lines, with confidence in my identity and without fear. I not only learned more about his viewpoint, but I also found that one of his critiques of my beliefs was pretty well-taken and I've used it to sharpen my own ideas. When it was all said and done, I had a better sense of this pastor's good and caring heart, felt closer to him and loved him more than I did before I watched the sermon. And aren't those some of the significant goals of unity?

The friend who suggested that I watch the sermon was shocked to hear that I actually followed through on my promise. He probably thought that I wax poetic about this unity stuff but fail to actually live it when put to the test. Little did he know! And if the well-known pastor ever wants to return the gesture and earnestly listen to my thoughts on the issue, I'd be down for that. After all, we live in the same city.

My friends David Sherman and Heejung Kim have spent a great deal of their careers studying self-affirmation theory in the context of groups. They've found that when people do self-affirmation exercises, they are much less likely to fall prey to the group-serving biases (e.g., overestimating your group's contributions to successful collaborative projects) that I discussed earlier in this chapter. They also found that self-affirmation exercises enable group members to accept and receive constructive criticism about their group without getting overly defensive. And most recently, they've found that self-affirmation exercises reduce ideological closed-mindedness and inflexibility when two groups are discussing issues with each other. Quite simply, we must affirm who we really are as the people of God before we can begin to interact with each other as the people of God.

Chapter 6 Questions

1. What did you think about the results of the Fein and Spencer study that looked at perceptions of Jewish versus non-Jewish women? Were the results surprising?

2. How do you think your group memberships affect your identity and self-esteem?

3. How do you think your perceptions of other groups in the body of Christ affect your self-esteem?

4. Which group memberships inform your identity the most? How do you know?

5. What sorts of group-serving biases do you see yourself or others falling prey to?

6. Are you reluctant to admit that certain groups in the body of Christ have something to teach you? What do you think this means?

7. What kinds of self-affirmation exercises would you do in order to prepare to listen to diverse viewpoints? What prayers would you pray? What Scripture passages would you meditate on?

7

Culture Wars

How Cultural Threat Leads to Hostile Conflict

O*ne of my friends is a Dallas-area pastor* who sometimes posts provocative questions on his Facebook page in order to stimulate discussion. Recently he asked the following question: "What should the church's attitude be toward 'illegal' aliens?" Not surprisingly, the question garnered 118 responses over just a few short hours.

The discussion began with a few people politely and thoughtfully presenting opposing viewpoints. However, it quickly got ugly as respondents began to make pejorative statements like, *"It's a no brainer!!!!"* that imply that those who disagree are simply stupid; careless statements such as, *"Lead 'em to the Lord and then deport 'em!"* that merely stalled the discussion and incited emotions; and self-righteous statements such as, *"Is this not a question just of Christian ethics . . . but also what THE BIBLE ACTUALLY SAYS??? Let us as Christians set a good example and follow what the Bible says instead of emotions. How 'bout that?"* that accused people with differing opinions of ignoring biblical teaching.

The discussion became so vitriolic that my pastor friend was forced to intervene like a schoolyard monitor, threatening to delete comments that weren't thoughtful and polite. What began as a simple difference in opinion swiftly devolved into something much darker.

Obviously, Facebook is the worst place ever for respectful discourse. However, the hostility displayed on my friend's Facebook page is similar to the hostility displayed during disagreements in lab experiments and in the real world. Why are difference and disagreement often tainted with hostility?

As we already know, categorizing and identity processes, if left unchecked, lead us to misperceive and derogate other cultural groups in the body of Christ. However, these processes do not work alone; they are often aggravated by group conflict processes. In the end, the mere existence of difference and disagreement between groups snowballs into outright hostility. As we begin to see other groups in the body of Christ as the enemy, we end up attacking them from our Facebook pages, our pulpits and our hearts.

This is particularly true when we disagree on Christian beliefs and practices. In my work with churches, I find that most Christians agree that we should unite across ethnic, linguistic and socioeconomic lines but *only* if we share beliefs and practices with the other. As soon as unity requires that we reconsider how we think about faith or how we express faith, we stall.

We tend to have a difficult time seeing groups with different perspectives as family members who offer invaluable resources and insight. Instead, we see their perspectives as less valuable, less important and less correct than our own. Armed with the belief that our faith perspective is entirely right, we easily come up with reasons why other perspectives aren't valuable and why dissenting voices should be extinguished. I mean, how dare they disagree with us, with Truth?

Indeed, it seems that when we discuss groups who have the audacity to differ from us in belief and practice, we're more likely to use the label *heretics* than the labels *brothers* and *sisters*. In doing so, we fail to consider the possibility that our interaction with other groups in the body of Christ can lead to mutual teaching and learning. Research on group conflict processes can help us understand why the mere existence of difference and disagreement between groups not only prevents us from valuing other perspectives but also often snowballs into outright hostility. Like categorizing and identity issues, conflict processes occur mostly outside of our awareness; when we become aware of them, we can see the role that they play in our interactions with different groups.

What Texas Football Can Tell Us About Conflict

I recently watched a television show called *Friday Night Lights* on Netflix. It's a show about the Dillon Panthers, a larger-than-life high school football team and the town that lives, eats and breathes Panther football. The show doesn't have a ton of fans, but I like it. There are pretty realistic football sequences, beautiful thirty-year-olds who play high school kids on the show and plenty of melo-drama. It's kind of like watching *SportsCenter* and *Dawson's Creek* at the same time. What's not to love? Besides, the Dillon Panthers display lots of fascinating group processes, and my inner nerd just can't resist a show about group processes.

The citizens of Dillon attend church on Sundays, but they *worship* on Friday nights at the football stadium. All of the grown-up men proudly wear the state championship rings that they earned when they were Panthers. Everyone in the Texas town goes to all the games, not just the playoff games. (Southern California people who watch the show are probably thinking, "Wait, there are actual games *before* the playoffs?") Coach Taylor's job is on the line every single Friday night because the entire town is living vicari-ously through the team. The team's undefeated record doesn't suffice. Coach must win *this Friday* or else the boosters will be calling for his head. To make matters worse, tensions in the town are running high because the team's All-American quarterback was recently injured, is now permanently paralyzed and is virtually irreplaceable. (That's a plot "twist" that surprised no one. What Hollywood sports story *doesn't* involve a star player getting hurt?)

In one episode, the Dillon Panthers are preparing to play their league rivals, the hated Arnett Mead Tigers. The stakes are high. Can the Panthers beat the Tigers? Will Coach Taylor get fired? Can the new QB handle the pressure?

The Panthers are serious about winning the game. This is made clear by the amount of time they spend practicing, analyzing videotape and strategizing. However, a few days before the game the Panthers discover that the Tigers have infiltrated and trashed the Panther locker room, destroying benches, uniforms and trophies, and spray painting obscenities on the walls. The Panthers are justifiably angry, but the honorable Coach Taylor warns them not to retaliate. Rather, he encourages them to dispense payback on the football field when they play the Tigers in the upcoming game. Naturally, the players completely ignore Coach's warning and plan to repay the Tigers immediately. (And really, who can blame them? They carry the honor of the entire town of Dillon on their thirty-year-old—er, fifteen-year-old—shoulders.) The next night, a group of players locate the Tigers quarterback's home and use baseball bats to demolish his vintage Mustang. Not the classiest move, but certainly very effective. Of course the Tigers strike back by attacking the new Panthers quarterback with so much vengeance that he lands in the hospital.

The interesting thing about this whole scenario is that football is practically an afterthought. The Panthers and Tigers supposedly live for football but have become so impassioned by their mutual hatred that they seem to have forgotten about the true source of their rivalry: football. It's ironic that the majority of the battles that these football teams fight don't involve a football. Rather, they involve verbal insults, destruction of property and physical harm that lead to even greater social distance between the teams. How quickly group competition often devolves into something much darker.

Eagles vs. Rattlers

Muzafer Sherif's classic research on group conflict can help us understand why seemingly innocent group competition often spirals into far-reaching hostility and conflict. But first, it's worth noting that Sherif conducted most of his research in the 1950s and 1960s, when many scientists were intensely focused on obtaining knowledge at any cost and not so focused on treating participants in an ethical manner. Finally in the 1970s, the United States government intervened and instituted ethical regulations. But good old Sherif carried out his research before any of the laws were in place, which helps to explain how he managed to conduct the brilliant but completely unethical experiment that I am about to describe.

Sherif had a hunch that group competition for scarce resources was a significant cause of group hostility and prejudice. He believed that this was most likely to occur when groups competed for an important goal that can only be attained by one group at the expense of the other group. In order to test this idea, he convinced a group of unsuspecting parents to let their eleven-year-old sons attend a summer camp at Robbers Cave State Park in Oklahoma. The parents and boys had no idea that the "camp" was actually a social psychology experiment on group hostility. (This would never happen today. Thank God for government regulations. And helicopter parents.) Before the camp, Sherif checked to make sure that none of the boys knew each other and that they all came from similar, well-adjusted homes. On the first day of the experiment, Sherif divided the boys into two groups and then transported them to the camp in separate buses. When the boys arrived at the camp, Sherif ensured that the two groups remained apart by assigning them to cabins at opposite ends of the park.

During the first week of camp, Sherif simply wanted the boys in each group to bond with the other boys in their respective group. As such, the two groups had zero contact with each other. Instead, the boys in each group participated in typical lighthearted camp activities like swimming, pitching tents and hiking. Each group also chose a name, made a team flag and stenciled the group name on their T-shirts. One group called itself the Rattlers; the other group called itself the Eagles. So far, everybody was having a fabulous time.

At the start of the second week of camp, the Rattlers and Eagles met each other for the first time and competed in friendly contests like baseball and tug of war. Sherif ensured that the stakes were high by offering valuable (at least in the eyes of eleven-year-old boys) prizes like trophies and pocketknives. The groups ate together in a common dining hall where the prizes were kept on display. During the meals, Sherif (who was posing as the camp handyman so that he could observe the boys without drawing attention to himself) noticed that the contests were producing strong feelings of prejudice and hostility toward the other group. At first, the boys were simply calling each other names like "stinkers" and "sissies." (How *Leave It to Beaver* of them.)

However, within a day, the boys began acting in more mean-spirited, physically aggressive ways. When the Eagles lost their first baseball game, they burned the Rattlers' flag. The leader of the Eagles even taunted the Rattlers, proudly declaring, "You can tell those guys I did it . . . I'll fight 'em." Predictably, the Rattlers burned the Eagles' flag in retaliation. When the Eagles won a game of tug of war, the Rattlers accused the Eagles of cheating and then raided their cabin, causing extensive damage including overturned beds and ripped mosquito netting. Completely lacking in creativity, the Eagles responded by invading the Rattlers' cabin. The Eagles also began collecting rocks to throw at the Rattlers. (How *Friday Night Lights* of them.)

The Eagles ultimately won the tournament. But it's not surprising that almost as soon as the Eagles paraded the trophies back to their cabin, the Rattlers stole them. Explosive fighting ensued. Fortunately, at this point in the experiment Sherif and the other researchers decided that it was time to intervene. (They spent an entire week attempting to restore peace between the Rattlers and Eagles with varying results.) By the end, Sherif noted that a naive observer would have thought the boys were "wicked, disturbed, and vicious." Within a matter of days, normal, well-adjusted, pleasant boys had become unrecognizably hostile.

Despite its obvious ethical limitations, the Robbers Cave experiment and others like it gave rise to *realistic conflict theory*, an important and useful theory about group conflict. According to this theory, relationships between groups get ugly when groups find themselves in a realistic conflict—a conflict in which they are competing for scarce resources. It all begins when two groups find themselves intensely vying for an important resource (or prize) that only one group can possess. At this point, each group will start to believe that it is more deserving of the resource than the other group. In order to justify this belief, it will name (or invent) all the reasons why the other group is less deserving of the resource. This is when groups start calling each other stinkers and sissies or names that are far worse. You can probably imagine how this line of thinking rapidly spirals into outright prejudice toward the other group. Ultimately, the name-calling and derogation turn into a darker hostility that dominates situations that have little to do with the original battle. And greater social distance between the groups is created and sustained.

This entire process is dizzying. As the Rattlers and Eagles demonstrated, even groups who have no history of negative interaction can swiftly become antagonistic when the goals are important enough. On *Friday Night Lights*, dominance on the football field (and the associated community pride) was the important goal that raised the stakes, turning what was originally a friendly league football game into a hostile conflict.

Group Conflict in the Real World

It turns out that realistic conflict occurs in the real world, beyond the boundaries of unethical psychology experiments and Hollywood stories. Researchers have found that between 1880 and 1930, the lynching of African Americans increased when cotton prices decreased in the South. This is most likely due to the fact that white and black farmers were competing for the same resource: money earned from the sale of cotton. When the resource became scarce (i.e., cotton prices dropped and profits decreased), the stakes were raised. In this case, the hostility became so great that it led to lynchings. More recently, research has demonstrated that discrimination toward immigrant groups increases when unemployment levels are high. When everyone is vying for a small number of jobs, people are less tolerant of immigrants. When we care enough about something, be it as trivial as a football game or as crucial as our livelihoods, the stakes are raised. And this is when things can start to get ugly.

I bet you know where I'm going with this, this being a book about divisions in the church and all. Perhaps you're wondering how realistic conflict could possibly contribute to barriers between different church groups. *Eleven-year-olds and football crazies and racists might get caught up in this realistic conflict stuff*, you say, *but I could care less about silly camp prizes and football and I certainly have never lynched anyone.* You're right. I probably wouldn't fight for camp prizes either. And even those of us who love our football teams have a tough time imagining ourselves taking a baseball bat to the other team's quarterback's car. And let's hope that none of us has even considered lynching anyone. But it's all relative, right? We all have camp prizes and football pride and lifestyles (read: beliefs and practices) about which we are quite passionate and for which we might even be willing to fight.

One of the many things I love about the body of Christ is that its members are passionate about God. We desire to know God and to love and represent him well in the world. As a result, we are a people who ardently live for our theology, values and practical applications of faith. In spite of our busy schedules and limited checking accounts, we devote significant resources to studying the Bible, attending conferences and retreats and even seminary, reading books, deepening friendship with other members of the body of Christ and intentionally seeking to represent Christ as we interact with the physical world. We recognize that it is important to possess accurate theology and to live authentic lives of faith; our investment of time, energy and money tends to reflect this recognition.

My brother John is someone who cares deeply about his relationship with God and engages in ministry with an unbelievable passion. As a full-time seminary student, he is able to spend the vast majority of his time praying, studying Scripture and theological views, and volunteering at his church. Basically, he is a monk.

The best thing about John is that in addition to being passionate, he is quite skilled at weaving theology into every single conversation. I know this because last summer at a party we attended, he engaged almost everyone in theological discussions. Theology and practical applications of faith are John's top priorities. Although all of us may not spend entire parties engrossed in intense theological discussions (I, for one, was far more engrossed in the s'mores I was eating), many of us would agree that theology and practical applications of faith are also our top priorities.

Interestingly, even though we all agree that it is important to possess accurate theology and lead authentic lives of faith, we don't agree on what this looks like. Further, the stakes are pretty high. We tend to care. We tend to be invested. We tend to believe that we have dutifully done our homework. We tend to be convinced that we possess the most accurate view. We tend to believe that our view should be the only view. All of these tendencies inevitably set the stage for a realistic conflict. However, rather than drawing near to each other for earnest and respectful conversation, we often follow in the footsteps of the Eagles and Rattlers.

Once we realize that the stakes are high and that only one viewpoint can prevail, we must justify our belief that our viewpoint is most deserving of victory. Before long, we are focusing on (or worse, inventing) negative traits about the other group that support our case. "Those people are heretics, dense, arrogant, ridiculous, not real Christians" and so forth—whatever helps us conclude that we're the only ones who possess truth. In the end, a conflict that could have been confined to a series of godly and meaningful discussions becomes characterized by a hostile mistrust that widens the divide between the groups. This sets the stage for antagonistic, competitive relationships with culturally different Christians that is made worse by our natural tendency to see different cultures as threatening.

High Cultural Threat Levels

Michael Zarate and colleagues studied how nationals are culturally threatened by immigrants. When people were asked to consider the possibility of sharing a community with immigrants who *differed* in language and interpersonal style, they felt threatened and responded with negative emotions. However, when they were asked to consider the possibility of sharing a community with immigrants who possessed the *same* language and interpersonal style, they were not at all threatened and did not respond negatively. Mere cultural difference provoked hostility even when ethnic difference did not. Apparently, we don't like it when culturally different people pollute our sacred culture with their different language and style.

Why do cultural threats trigger such strong reactions from us? We'll look at three causes in particular. First, cultural threats increase ambiguity, which is unfortunate because we hate ambiguity. Second, cultural threats can confuse us, especially when they are caused by people who are supposed to be members of our group.

Third, cultural threats are threatening because we fear negative consequences more than we seek positive outcomes.

We hate ambiguity. Whether we are trained in psychology or not, we have a strong need to make sense of our world, a strong need to know and understand what is going on around us. If we understand the world around us, we have a far greater chance of controlling it. Even if we can't control our world, understanding can help us to make informed choices about what to do next. So we are constantly analyzing situations, trying to predict the behavior of others and pinpoint answers to questions such as *Who am I?* and *What is my purpose?* We have a strong need to know and a strong need to eliminate uncertainty.

Arie Kruglanski has devoted his career to studying the lengths to which humans will go in order to avoid ambiguity. He studies a phenomenon called our *need for cognitive closure*, which is defined as an individual's "need for a firm answer to a question, any firm answer as opposed to confusion and/or ambiguity."

Because we're uncomfortable with ambiguity, if we can find a concept to help us make sense of the world, we will cling to it—even if the concept is incomplete. We want to quickly close the door to ambiguity because it threatens who we are. In our brazen attempts to make sense of the world, we prefer to settle for *an* answer even if it's not *the* answer. When we encounter different cultural perspectives, the number of possible "answers" is increased and so is ambiguity. Naturally, we want to squelch those pesky different perspectives.

Our need for cognitive closure can also help explain why we are resistant to Christian beliefs and practices that stem from different cultural groups. For example, theologian Scot McKnight uses the concept of atonement to illustrate how we are often divided by our different faith perspectives. In his book *A Community Called Atonement*, he presents various atonement metaphors—offering, justification, reconciliation, redemption and ransom—and shows that the abundance of metaphors typically leads to division because groups think that their particular metaphor provides the entire or most important truth about atonement and that other groups' metaphors are wrong or relatively less important.

McKnight points out that it is quite ironic that the body of Christ is ardently divided over the definition of atonement—a concept that is relational and unifying *by definition*. Research on the need for cognitive closure helps to explain why our church group, when trying to make sense of a difficult and mysterious concept such as atonement, might cling to one metaphor of atonement and resist acceptance of other metaphors. To acknowledge that other useful metaphors might exist is to risk opening what we have already cognitively closed.

Kruglanski and colleagues have found that some individuals are naturally higher or lower in need for cognitive closure. Individuals who have a high need for closure tend to agree with statements such as "I think that having clear rules and order at work is essential to success" and "I do not like situations that are uncertain." These people tend to disagree with statements like "Even after I've made up my mind about something, I am always eager to consider a different opinion" and "I like to have friends who are unpredictable."

According to Kruglanski, "A strong need for closure is experienced as a desire to have closure urgently and maintain it permanently. Hence, individuals with a strong need for closure tend to 'seize' on information permitting a judgment on a topic of interest and to 'freeze' on such judgment, becoming relatively impermeable or closed-minded to further relevant information." Individuals who have a strong need for cognitive closure tend to favor tidy answers (even if they are incomplete answers) over true answers that are perhaps a bit abstract and untidy.

People with a strong need for cognitive closure aren't stupid, they just have a higher need to predict and control the world around them. It makes the world seem more safe, predictable and understandable.

Lest we decide that we're not one of *those* people who are high in need for closure and that this research isn't applicable to us, we should pay attention to the fact that Kruglanski has also found that certain situations can make people more likely to crave cognitive closure, regardless of their natural tendency toward or against cognitive closure. All people are more likely to succumb to need for cognitive closure when they believe that the benefits of premature closure outweigh the costs of remaining open-minded.

Naturally, group situations often trigger a high need for closure. Because we want to maintain solid ingroup/outgroup boundaries, we may cling to our beliefs and remain closed to other points of view even when it simply does not make sense to do it. If the goal is to maintain psychological distance from the group we have vilified, we will cling to any ideological beliefs that differentiate us from that group. But remember, we often invent or exaggerate ingroup/outgroup distinctions to the point that a distinction that was barely a blip on our radar suddenly becomes a huge deal.

We hate black sheep. The second reason cultural threats are so threatening is the *black sheep effect*. Cultural distinctions are so crucial to maintaining ingroup/outgroup boundaries that group members have a special hatred for other ingroup members who, for the most part, act like normal ingroup members but do not "toe the party line" on one or two important issues. This black sheep effect helps to explain why group members go to great lengths to punish and exclude other ingroup members who do not subscribe to the cultural beliefs of the group.

Examples of black sheep are a pro-choice Republican and a pro-death-penalty Democrat. For the most part, the individual buys into the majority ideology, but fails to toe the party line when it comes to one issue. Yeah, we hate those people.

As ingroup members who disagree on one or two issues, black

sheep blur the cultural lines that separate the ingroup and the out-group. For this great offense, ingroup members hate black sheep and reserve their worst judgment for them. In fact, studies show that ingroup members treat black sheep worse than they treat out-group members.

Outgroup members are *supposed to disagree* with us. As such, we are not as threatened by their disagreement. If anything, their dis-agreement with us further solidifies ingroup/outgroup boundaries by showing us that *we* are different from *them*. Ingroup members, on the other hand, are *supposed to agree* with us, so we are shocked and appalled if they express disagreement. Further, the fact that they disagree with us blurs the ideological lines between the two groups. If one of our group members agrees with *them* on this im-portant issue, then maybe *we* are not so different from *them* after all. The mere thought of this makes us feel angry and threatened.

Recently my colleagues and I conducted a series of experiments that suggest ingroup members who interact with those they perceive to be black sheep experience negative physiological and psycho-logical changes. Basically, ingroup members' bodies instinctually began to prepare for a fight-or-flight situation when they interacted with black sheep. Specifically, ingroup members showed significant increases in heart rate, blood pressure, cardiac output (the volume of blood being pumped out of the heart and out to the body) and vaso-dilation (the arteries opening up to accommodate the increased blood flow) when they interacted with black sheep. They were ready to rumble—with their own ingroup members! However, when in-group members interacted with outgroup members, they did not show these fight-or-flight physiological changes.

As far as psychological changes go, ingroup members who inter-acted with black sheep were more confrontational, expressing a greater desire to persuade, confront or scold the black sheep. However, they were much less confrontational when asked to in-teract with an outgroup member. Perhaps most importantly, we found that the fight-or-flight response and confrontational attitude that ingroup members exhibited toward black sheep were especially likely to occur when the ingroup members believed that they possessed "issue-relevant knowledge"—in other words, when they believed that they were expert group members who could rightfully determine who should or should not be in the group.

As we know from chapter 4, due to categorizing and the biases it creates, just about any group member is likely to believe that they are expert group members. Remember the biker study? Both the sport bikers and chopper bikers fell prey to the gold standard effect, believing that their respective subgroups represented the most important, relevant and prototypical characteristics of the larger, common group of all bikers. Essentially, these two groups decided that their perspective was the only one that mattered and that they did not need to listen to or value the perspective of the other group.

Within the context of the larger body of Christ, when we interact with fellow Christians who possess a different cultural viewpoint or tradition, we are often interacting with what we perceive to be black sheep. Due to the gold standard effect, we believe that our culturally influenced beliefs and practices are the best ones and that our cultural group should be the standard against which all other cultural groups are measured. As a result of this thinking, anyone who disagrees with us is perceived as someone who is failing to live up to the cultural group's standards—a black sheep.

The mere existence of these so-called black sheep threatens to blur what we perceive to be the important beliefs and practices that differentiate Christians from everyone else. Rather than remaining cognitively open to our culturally different fellow followers of Christ who might offer a much-needed perspective, we dig our heels in and seek cognitive closure. In doing so, we tell ourselves that these people are black sheep who deserve the black sheep treatment—and we are happy to oblige by calling them heretics.

According to research on cognitive closure and the black sheep effect, when faced with a different cultural viewpoint, we're inclined to cling to our existing beliefs and reject the perspectives and wisdom of the outgroup, even when it might make sense to open up and learn. In other words, we tend to separate ourselves from the rest of the body. Unfortunately, our insistence upon cognitive closure is inconsistent with the reality of knowing Christ (and all of his mysteries) and being part of a body that by definition possesses different viewpoints that don't necessarily lead to a tidy answer.

We fear negative consequences. The third reason cultural threats are so threatening is that we fear negative outcomes. Pastor and theologian Greg Boyd writes, "What does truth have to fear? I sometimes wonder if the animosity some express toward [those who offer a different perspective] is motivated by the fear that the case [for the opposing perspective] might turn out to be more compelling than they can handle."

We're afraid that *they* might influence *us* in negative ways. As a result, our crosscultural interactions are not characterized by humility, openness, interdependence and hopeful invitation. Rather, they are characterized by fear, retreat into cognitive closure and accusations. Within our culture of fear, our words and behavior are motivated by a desire to avoid being like a certain group, rather than a desire to be like Jesus.

E. Tory Higgins, a social psychologist who studies the self and motivation, makes a distinction between prevention and promotion orientation that can help to explain the culture of fear in the body of Christ. Basically, Higgins believes that people are motivated by promotion (achieving a lofty ideal or advancement) or by prevention (avoiding danger or negative consequences).

The promotion-oriented student, for example, is motivated to study for an exam in order to obtain a good grade. Her motivation to study is driven by positivity and hope for achievement. On the contrary, the prevention-oriented student is motivated to study for an exam in order to avoid getting a poor grade. The motivation to study is driven by negativity and fear of failure.

Both promotion and prevention orientations are powerful motivation tools; they can both lead to high performance. However, Higgins has found that promotion is related to eagerness (a sensitivity to and desire for positive outcomes), whereas prevention is related to vigilance (a sensitivity to and avoidance of negative outcomes). In other words, promotion-oriented people are eager to find positive things so they can obtain them, while prevention-oriented people are eager to find negative things so they can avoid them.

The body of Christ seems to be plagued with a pervasive prevention orientation. We have a heightened sensitivity to what we perceive to be the negative happenings in the church, and we are especially vigilant in tracking those happenings. It doesn't take long for us to identify a negative happening, and once we do, we use strong language to motivate people to avoid it. This creates a culture of fear in which we're constantly looking for (real or imagined) threats and then orienting our lives around avoiding them.

Preachers often build sermons around this avoidance of threat. They construct theological arguments by talking about what another church group is doing/thinking and why we shouldn't be like them.

The other day, I listened to a podcast of an internationally known pastor—let's call him Pastor Aaron. Even though his sermon was on the holiness of God, he prefaced it by saying that during his commute to church that morning he had listened to a sermon of a nearby pastor—Pastor Brian. Pastor Aaron didn't say much about Pastor Brian's sermon other than to point out that Pastor Brian failed to mention the name of Jesus during the fifteen-minute portion of the sermon that Pastor Aaron happened to hear during his commute.

Based on this limited data, Pastor Aaron sarcastically concluded that even though Pastor Brian probably loves Jesus, he "hides it well." The congregation laughed. Pastor Aaron went on to declare that at *his* church they know that Jesus reigns supreme—the implication being that Pastor Brian's church is misguided and should be avoided. Rather than simply teaching his congregants about the holiness of God, Pastor Aaron used sarcasm to subtly but powerfully scare them into following him. He might as well have added, "If you don't stick with this church, you'll end up like Pastor Brian— a barely Christian person that we will mock."

Pastor Aaron seems to have been operating from a prevention orientation. He vigilantly tracked the negative event (Pastor Brian's failure to mention the name of Jesus) and swiftly (perhaps too swiftly) concluded that people like Pastor Brian, as perpetrators of negative events, are to be avoided. Then he perpetuated the culture of fear by passing this orientation on to his large body of listeners.

Imagine how differently Pastor Aaron would have felt if he had approached Pastor Brian's sermon with a promotion orientation. He probably would have been encouraged and challenged by Pastor Brian's words. He probably also would have cut Pastor Brian some slack for not mentioning Jesus' name at fifteen-minute intervals.

Researchers have found evidence for a trait negativity bias: humans have a tendency to pay more attention to and place more value on negative information than positive information. In our minds one bad trait can easily override numerous good traits and destroy a person's reputation. (This is why negative political ads are so influential.) In addition, Tiffany Ito and others have found that "negative information weighs more heavily on the brain." In their study, they attached electrodes to participants' scalps and recorded participants' brain activity while they viewed slides depicting positive images (e.g., a red Ferrari, people enjoying a roller coaster ride), negative images (e.g., a mutilated face, a handgun pointed at the camera) or neutral images (e.g., a plate, a hair dryer). Not surprisingly, the researchers found that brain activity was more pronounced when participants were viewing negative images as opposed to positive or neutral images.

From a survival perspective, it makes sense for people to stay alert to negative information; in order to stay safe, you need to be aware of the dangers. However, from a kingdom perspective, it is adaptive for members of the body of Christ to stay alert to positive information about others. In order to stay unified, we need to override our natural tendency to focus on what we perceive to be negative information about other groups and instead stay alert to the positive information that they bring to the table of faith.

If we're going to be vigilant about anything, we should be vigilant about the positive things that God is doing through our fellow members. In other words, we need to be promotion oriented. Our default orientation should be one of eagerness to see God working, eagerness to see God glorified in those around us, eagerness to live as the unified body of Christ.

What Now?

At the moment, we tend to see culturally different Christians as our opponents in the realistic conflict for truth, influence and other "scarce" resources. Our competitive relationship with other Christians is made even more antagonistic by our penchant for negativity and natural hatred for ambiguity and black sheep. Not only are we competing against them, but the mere existence of them causes us so much discomfort that we pay special attention to the ways that they *might* be hurting us. I say "might" because we are often more threatened by what they might do (the so-called slippery slope) than what they are actually doing right now. For this reason, we feel justified in holding them at arm's length and drawing closer to our homogenous group.

The glaring problem here is that our definition of *we* is far too small—it includes those who are part of our homogenous group and excludes everyone else in the diverse body of Christ. Research shows that whether we include people in our group or not determines how threatening we perceive them to be. In a research article

titled "When You and I Are 'We,' 'You' Are Not Threatening," Wendi
Gardner and colleagues found that individuals are much less likely
to perceive another person as a threatening competitor if they perceive that person to be an ingroup member instead of an outgroup
member. When we perceive culturally different Christians as fellow
members of the body of Christ, we will be less likely to perceive
them as threatening competitors.

Indeed, when we adopt an inclusive identity, we are more likely
to see how other groups can help us and are more willing to receive
constructive criticism from them. Matthew Hornsey and colleagues
found that Anglo Australian participants (the ingroup) were more
likely to receive constructive criticism from Asian Australians (the
outgroup) when Asian Australians were perceived as fellow
members of a shared, inclusive identity (Australians).

Specifically, Anglo Australians were more open to receiving
critical information on the injustices that Asian Australians experienced in Australian society when they perceived Asian Australians
as part of their group. (This finding might be the key to helping
privileged Christians receive critical information about the injustices that less privileged Christians experience in American society
and church, but we'll save that conversation for chapter 9.) By perceiving Asian Australians as ingroup members rather than outgroup
members, Anglo Australians were able to set aside their fear of ambiguity, relax their competitive stance and adopt a promotion orientation that enabled them to lean in to hear from a culturally different viewpoint, rather than recoil in fear. Ultimately and beautifully,
the Anglo Australians found that when the outgroup is a friend
rather than a foe, defensiveness is no longer necessary.

As we begin to change the way we see ourselves—through
adopting more inclusive language, doing self-affirmation exercises
that remind us of common membership in the body of Christ and
overriding the effects of natural categorizing—we will begin to see
that *they* are a part of *us*. Once *they* become *us*, *they* will no longer

be threatening and like the Anglo Australians in the study we will be able to set aside our fear of ambiguity, relax our competitive stance and adopt a promotion orientation that enables us to lean in to hear from a culturally different viewpoint, rather than recoil in fear.

Chapter 7 Questions

1. What are some examples of realistic conflicts in the church today?

2. What types of emotions do you experience when you find yourself caught up in one of these realistic conflicts?

3. How do you perceive Christians who are on the other side of the realistic conflict?

4. Who would you call "black sheep" Christians? What characteristics do they have?

5. Do you think you have more of a promotion or prevention orientation toward culturally different Christians?

6. What steps can you take to adopt more of a promotion orientation toward culturally different Christians?

7. 1 John 4:18 says, "There is no fear in love. But perfect love drives out fear, because fear has to do with punishment. The one who fears is not made perfect in love." How do you think this verse relates to this chapter?

8

Blinded by Culture

How Our Culture Clouds Our Judgment

My friend Randy is a history professor at a Christian college. In many ways he holds to the history professor stereotype: white-haired, intelligent, respectable and a little stodgy. However, he is unique in that he begins every class session by leading his students in a rousing rendition of one of the old European church hymns. This practice stems from Randy's belief that young Christians have "issues" because they possess bad theology. He is remedying this problem one class session at a time by teaching his students accurate theology via hymns—because according to him, that is where real theology always has and always will lie.

Not long ago, Randy invited ten of his students over to his house for dinner. Before the meal commenced, he attempted to lead the students in the Doxology ("Praise God, From Whom All Blessings Flow") that is most often used in his conservative, Eurocentric faith tradition. Much to his shock and dismay, he discovered that only one of his ten students knew the words to the brief hymn.

He responded by interrogating them about the churches they attended and how they had lived as Christians without knowing this important piece of the Christian faith. He then sent me and a few others a forceful email demanding to know whether "this lack of knowledge represents an institutional problem for [his Christian college]? A problem for the Christian Church? A problem for both?" He honestly believed that his students' unfamiliarity with an old, Eurocentric hymn posed a threat not only to his particular Christian college but also to the worldwide church! Plus, he believed that the threat warranted an antagonistic response.

Randy failed to capitalize on the group's diversity by creating an opportunity for crosscultural sharing. Rather than graciously sharing his predinner prayer tradition with the students and then inviting them to respond by sharing their own traditions, he put his students at arm's length, convinced that he had good reason to do so.

When Realistic Conflict and Cultural Threat Collide

Sometimes what we perceive to be a realistic conflict is in fact a cultural threat. We believe that we are fighting the good fight for an immutable truth, when in fact we are simply waging war against a cultural threat, a different perspective that threatens ours.

To be clear, I'm not suggesting that all Christian truth is culturally relative. Rather, I'm pointing out that it is easy for us to follow in the footsteps of my friend Randy and confuse culturally based faith perspectives and traditions with universal Christian truth. Randy was convinced that individuals who do not know "important" hymns pose a serious threat to the church because they do not possess "accurate" theology. Unfortunately, Randy was unaware of the ways in which his particular cultural tradition greatly influenced his faith perspectives and values. Naturally, he believed that his perspective was a necessary and universal one and was intolerant of those who possessed a different perspective. Much like Randy the Hymn Lover, we often charge into what we think is a worthwhile realistic conflict for the sole possession of truth when in fact it is simply a cultural difference that should not threaten us.

There are two reasons why it is extremely easy to do this.

The similarity of religion and culture. Religion and culture are easily confused because they seem to work in very similar ways; definitions of religion and culture are eerily similar. Psychology textbook authors typically define culture as "a system of enduring meanings, beliefs, values, assumptions, institutions, and practices shared by a large group of people and transmitted from one generation to another."

Compare that with sociologist Emile Durkheim's classic definition of religion: a "unified system of beliefs and practices relative to sacred things, that is to say, things set apart and forbidden—beliefs and practices which united into one single moral community called a Church, all those who adhere to them." Durkheim's definition of religion is basically a definition of culture that focuses on the sacred.

It gets better! Anthropologist Clifford Geertz's definition of religion is also similar to common understandings of culture: religion is "(1) a system of symbols which acts to (2) establish powerful, pervasive, and long-lasting moods and motivations in men by (3) formulating conceptions of a general order of existence and (4) clothing those conceptions with such an aura of factuality that (5) the moods and motivations seem uniquely realistic."

These definitions suggest that religion and culture operate in extremely similar ways; both create symbols, meanings, languages and practices that unify and organize groups of people over an extended period of time. No wonder we have a difficult time distinguishing between the two! Because religion and culture operate in similar ways, many researchers have begun to study religion *as* culture. Cultural psychologist Joni Sasaki and I have begun to study differences in Protestant groups and have found that religious beliefs influence and predict behavior much like cultural beliefs do.

But before I describe our study, I should say a word or two about ethical standards in psychology research. As you may have noticed, a fair amount of the research I've described in this book involves deception. Psychologists often use deception because the goal of research is to observe individuals' normal behavior. Unfortunately, it is impossible to conduct certain kinds of research without withholding information about some aspects of the research. For example, I wouldn't have been able to effectively observe the team processes in my teams research (described in chapter 5) if the participants in the study had known that their "teammates" were confederates who worked for me and were not real participants in the study. Also, sometimes it's necessary to misinform participants in order to get them to adopt certain attitudes or behaviors that are important to study. The good news is that research on the use of deception in psychological studies has revealed that, on average, participants don't seem to react negatively to being deceived. However, not surprisingly, the use of deception remains the most controversial ethical issue related to research.

Current ethical standards require that all research projects be approved by an institutional review board prior to the start of the data collection process. This board of community members and institution members checks to make sure that study participants will be treated ethically, that the benefits of the study outweigh the risks to participants, that the participants' privacy is maintained and so on. For good reason, researchers (such as myself) who want to use deception in their study must submit their study proposal to even more intensive ethical scrutiny by the institutional review board. Further, they must make the difficult case that no other methods for conducting research are available and that the deception will not influence people's decision to participate. In addition, whenever deception is used, the researcher must debrief participants after the experiment ends and inform them of the reasons for the deception, discuss any misconceptions they might have and remove any harmful effects of the deception. We ad-

hered to all of these ethical guidelines in the experiment I'm about
to describe.

As I mentioned earlier, Joni and I have studied how Protestant
religious beliefs affect and predict behavior much like cultural beliefs do. In our study, we led Calvinist and Arminian participants
to believe that they were moral failures, and then we looked to see
what this did to their self-esteem and self-awareness levels. (Who
ever said research is boring?) We discovered that after an experimenter suggested to Arminians that they were not living up to
their moral standard, their self-awareness spiked and their self-
esteem plummeted. But Calvinists didn't show any change in self-
awareness or self-esteem after it was suggested that they were not
living up to their moral standard.

Before you go assuming that Calvinists are indifferent to moral
failure or that Arminians are far too legalistic, consider the theological differences between Arminians and Calvinists. Generally
speaking, Arminians believe that salvation can be lost and Calvinists believe that salvation cannot be lost. Naturally, Arminians
were troubled to learn that they were not living up to their moral
standard because they believe that this can have serious ramifica-
tions on their salvation status. And naturally, Calvinists were free
from care because they believe that their salvation is secure. The
doctrine of the perseverance of the saints is looking pretty attractive right about now, isn't it?

(Consistent with ethical standards, after the study was over, we
debriefed the participants, explained that we had deceived them
for the purposes of research and assured them that we have no idea
whether they are a moral failure or not but that we love them all
the same.)

Just like cultural beliefs affect how people respond to certain
situations, religious beliefs can also affect how people respond to
certain situations. In our study, religious belief worked like cultural belief by affecting participants' perceptions of and response to

a certain situation—that is, their moral failure. This study shows that in many ways, religion operates like culture. For this reason, religion and culture are often confused.

The application of cultural tools to new contexts. It actually gets a bit more complicated. The confusion caused by the similarity of religion and culture is exacerbated because we not only use our cultural tools in the context in which we were born (such as language, social roles and so forth), but we also apply them to new and diverse contexts (such as worship style, religious traditions, biblical interpretation and the like). In this way, culture can greatly influence religious beliefs and practices.

For example, a person who is raised in a reserved and unemotional culture will automatically prefer worship practices that are reserved and unemotional, and avoid more exuberant or demonstrative practices. And due to the invisible nature of culture, this person can easily be influenced by culture without even knowing it. It's so easy to see how *their* culture is influencing *them*, but it's pretty difficult to see how *our* culture is influencing *us*. Culture is our modus operandi—anyone tracking us can see the cultural fingerprints that mark our religious beliefs and practices, but we lack the awareness to see it ourselves. All the more reason to develop crosscultural relationships with people who don't share our blind spots and can offer much-needed perspective on our culture.

In addition to influencing an individual's religious preferences, culture also influences organized religions. It's pretty clear that culture greatly influences Christianity from era to era. Just look at how Western perspectives on Christian faith have closely mirrored cultural changes in the West.

Philosopher Charles Taylor tracked the ways that Christian faith perspectives changed over time and found that before the Renaissance, Christian truth (that is, the idea of religious truth as laid out by Thomas Aquinas, *obviously*) was primarily applied to the entire cosmos (physical, spiritual and social), with much less focus on individual subjective experience. The idea of Christian truth began to change, however, during the Renaissance with an emphasis on reason and the view of the individual as the interpreter and judge of knowledge. This cultural shift, combined with the fact that scientific authorities were now making dramatic claims about the world, led theologians to focus on the individual subjective experience of faith, rather than broader, cosmic themes. Essentially, an individualistic emphasis in faith became the new standard of Christian faith. (Some people, such as church growth and evangelism professor Soong-Chan Rah, have made the case that the Western Christian individualism took root much earlier than the Renaissance.)

Cultural Idolatry in the Church

Clearly, the Western cultural value of individualism has dominated Western Christianity. Individualism has become so closely intertwined with Christianity that it is difficult to tell the two apart! Indeed, Rah devoted much of his book *The Next Evangelicalism* to discussing the ways in which Western culture and American Christianity have crisscrossed to the point of being indistinguishable. Rah rightly sees this as a significant problem and concludes by offering insight on how American Protestant churches can make a much-needed escape from Western culture.

Cultural psychologist Adam Cohen agrees that the stark individualism that plagues American society is probably hurting unity efforts in the worldwide church. Drawing from the apostle Paul's writings in Romans 12 and 1 Corinthians 12, Cohen writes, "The one, universal, worldwide community of Christians (the Church) is intended to hold itself accountable to its individual members and committed to a communitarian understanding of its mission. Perhaps because of its preference for individualistic, [emotional] motives, American Protestantism has not fully developed its doctrine of the Church."

Because culture and religion are so easily confused, many American Christians have automatically and unknowingly adopted a Western cultural viewpoint on Christian faith that significantly differs from other cultural viewpoints. This is a problem for crosscultural interactions in the church. Although American cultural values have dominated Christian faith, there are growing pockets of Christians who have been less influenced by American cultural values and more rooted in other cultural values. However, both groups believe that they are the gold standard and are convinced that their cultural perspective on faith should be adopted by the universal church. Before long, they are engaged in an overblown culture war that they are convinced is a realistic conflict. Let's look at cultural differences in individualism and collectivism as one stark example of the ways in which culture influences religion and sets the stage for cultural threats that are mistaken for realistic conflicts.

Cultural psychologists have studied cultural differences in individualism and collectivism for years. On the one hand, generally speaking, individualism is common in Western cultures, focuses on individuals as separate from the social context, values internal and private personal attributes, and emphasizes uniqueness, self-expression, individual goals and direct communication (e.g., "saying what's on your mind"). On the other hand, collectivism is common in Eastern cultures, focuses on the individual as inseparable from the social context, values external and public personal attributes, and emphasizes belongingness, fitting in, communal goals and indirect communication (e.g., "reading others' minds" in order to anticipate their needs). In the individualistic culture, "the squeaky wheel gets the grease," whereas in collectivistic culture, "the nail that stands out gets pounded down."

Because culture affects religion and vice versa, Christians who hail from individualistic cultures often emphasize and value an individual faith, whereas Christians from collectivistic cultures tend to emphasize and value a collectivistic, socially oriented faith. For example, studies show that individualistic Americans prefer internal and individualistic faith practices and agree with statements such as, "The prayers I say when I am alone carry as much meaning and personal emotion as those said by me during services." Individualistic American Christians are less likely to see more extrinsic and social faith practices as valuable and tend not to agree with statements that suggest that communal, ritual prayer is more powerful than individual prayer. As a result, collectivistic faith practices (typically seen in non-Western Christians as well as some Roman Catholic, Episcopal, Lutheran, American Baptist and Congregational congregations) are less valued and in some cases, not even considered legitimate Christianity.

The strong preference for more individualistic expressions of faith not only affects how much we value and legitimize different faith practices, but it also causes many crosscultural misunderstandings within the church. Differences in individualism and collectivism easily come up when different cultural groups discuss the past injustices that one group's ancestors heaped on the other group's ancestors. The Christian from the collectivist culture often says, "Your people did this to my people," whereas the Christian from the individualist culture often responds with, "I'm not responsible for what my grandparents did." The collectivist's socially oriented faith includes the possibility of social guilt and requires that individuals who are connected to oppressors be responsible for sins of oppression. However, the individualist's individual faith only knows individual guilt and is offended by the idea that one person can be held responsible for another person's actions.

In this case, both the collectivist and the individualist start from opposite departure points and often misunderstand why or how the other person can possibly maintain their beliefs and still call himself or herself Christian. In the end, what is perceived as a realistic conflict over the "truth" (e.g., the correct definition of guilt) is in fact simply a cultural difference that requires mutual understanding and sharing. In the end, both the individualists and collectivists are "correct" in the sense that they both present culturally based perspectives on guilt that offer an aspect of truth. Wellrounded Christian faith involves both individual and social responsibility. Once both cultural perspectives are shared and properly valued, individualists and collectivists can begin to work together to find an appropriate solution to the issue at hand. Without this mutual openness and understanding, the cultural disagreement will be perceived as a realistic conflict that further divides different cultural groups in the church.

In my work with Christian organizations, I have come across a curious trend. Pastors and leaders often launch diversity initiatives that are designed to attract minority participants, but when the minorities actually participate, all hell breaks loose. Increases in diversity are often met with more conflict, dissatisfaction with the organization across the board and disgruntled majority and minority participants. Ultimately, the pastors and leaders throw their hands in the air and give up, saying that the challenges of diversity outweigh the benefits. (I am saddened by how quickly they reach this conclusion, but that is a totally different issue.)

Research suggests that diversity initiatives are doomed to fail among Christian groups that idolize their cultural identities. Due to this idolatry, minority group members are not invited as valuable members of the all-inclusive *we* and their cultural perspectives are not seen as valuable and necessary. Rather, they are seen as threatening and wholly inaccurate simply because they are different from our idolized cultural perspectives. As a result, if they are invited to participate in the organization at all, they are invited to participate as *them*—subordinate "others" and second-class citizens who are bound to be dissatisfied. This is no good. Until we relativize our cultural identities and adopt an inclusive group identity, our diversity initiatives are doomed to failure because we will never fully appreciate our diverse brothers and sisters and they will not feel appreciated.

Cultural Idolatry in the Early Church

Culture's influence on religious beliefs and practices leads Christians to perceive realistic conflicts that do not actually exist and to keep culturally different Christians at bay. This is really frustrating. But it's comforting to know that when it comes to conflict, the contemporary church is probably no worse than the historical church. The early church had its share of realistic and cultural conflicts too.

Not long after Pentecost (an event that, among other things, served to unify an increasingly diverse church), the early church found itself divided over the issue of circumcision. One group, which comprised old-school Pharisees, believed that all new converts needed to be circumcised. These men had devoted their lives to studying and obeying the ancient law of Moses, which required circumcision. As far as they were concerned, the law of Moses needed to be upheld. End of discussion. However, the other group, which comprised new-school converts who weren't necessarily circumcised Jews, was adamantly opposed to this circumcision business. For one group, the ancient law was at stake. For the other group, private parts were at stake. (Even though I am not male, I can certainly empathize with the latter group. Adult circumcision with the use of first-century surgical techniques couldn't have been particularly appealing. Not that I'm choosing sides or anything.)

At any rate, the conflict escalated to the point that it caused a major division within the early church. The pro-circumcision group was essentially telling the pro-private-parts group that they could not call themselves followers of Christ unless they underwent the procedure. Things were becoming hostile. This is a classic case of perceiving a realistic conflict when it fact it was simply a cultural threat. Due to this misperception, the conflict quickly escalated.

Biblical scholar Robert Tannehill comments that this particular dispute was characterized by "considerable vehemence, threatening the unity between the Judean church and new mission areas," ultimately leading to "a major crisis" in the mission of the fledgling church. Recognizing the gravity of the situation, several apostles, including Paul, Barnabas and Peter stepped in to mediate. They called a meeting, brought the two groups together and let them hash it out. This did not go well. Rather than engaging in godly and humble discussion, they acted like Eagles and Rattlers. Basically, a lot of people were talking, but no one was listening to each other.

After a while, Peter finally stood up and reminded everyone of a couple of things. One, he reminded them that since they are not God, they don't necessarily have the authority to create rules for other followers of Christ. And two, he invoked their common membership in a far more meaningful, far more powerful group: the group of people who have experienced Christ's grace and have now devoted their lives to following in his gracious footsteps. Interestingly, invoking common group membership was one of the methods that Sherif used to help the Rattlers and Eagles reach a ceasefire. In fact, much research suggests that creating a common group identity is the key to overcoming the divisions caused by categorizing, identity and conflict processes.

After his speech, Peter invited Paul and Barnabas to tell everyone about all of the miraculous things that God was doing among the Gentiles (in spite of their intact private parts). Luke, the author of Acts, wrote that "the whole assembly became silent as they listened" (Acts 15:12). After being reminded of their common group membership, the two groups were finally able to listen to each other's unique cultural perspectives. Soon after that, they reconciled, reached out to the new Christians in unity and decided to cut them some slack.

What Now?

This can work for the modern church too. In fact, the entire next chapter is devoted to helping church groups forge a common group identity with groups that they previously held at bay.

From the very beginning, divisions have threatened the mission of the church. But it is also evident that from the very beginning, followers of Christ have demonstrated that they can overcome divisions in order to preserve and strengthen the mission. Clearly, we have the potential to be so engaged in our common identity as members of the body of Christ that we begin to treat each other as fellow ingroup members. The key to achieving a common ingroup identity is cross-cultural interaction. The next chapter is all about doing this right.

Chapter 8 Questions

1. Do you know anyone like Randy the Hymn Lover?

2. Do you see Randy the Hymn Lover in yourself? How so?

3. How do you see your culture influencing your religious beliefs and practices?

4. Think of a few cultural idioms (e.g., "Time flies" or "The squeaky wheel gets the grease"). How do you think these cultural idioms relate to religious beliefs and practices in your culture?

5. Why do you think it is difficult to see how your culture influences your religious beliefs and practices but much easier to see how other people's culture influences their beliefs and practices?

6. If you asked a culturally different person to assess how your culture influences your religious beliefs and practices, what do you think he or she would say?

7. What do you think about the notion that American Christianity is held captive by Western individualism?

8. How do you think that individualism hurts church unity? What can be done about this? What would it take for you to adopt a strong inclusive identity that helps you to value different cultural perspectives?

9

Creating Positive
Crosscultural Interactions

The two public high schools in my north Minneapolis neighborhood are longtime rivals. All things considered, the students at the schools are more similar than dissimilar: most are black, most come from low-income homes and most live in the neighborhood. Despite their similarity and the fact that the schools are located mere blocks apart from each other, the Henry High Patriots and North High Polar Bears can't stand each other. Naturally.

Last year, however, due to district-wide budget cuts and low enrollment at North High, the school board decided to combine the athletic programs at the two schools. As a result, all North High and Henry High volleyball players now compete as one team: the awkwardly named "North-Henry High Polar Bear Patriots." Unsurprisingly, all of the kids I know hated this arrangement initially. A few of the girls on the Henry volleyball team recently told me that at first, they were upset that North High players would be joining their team. "We thought that the North High girls would be b-----s who suck at volleyball," one of the girls admitted to me.

As the volleyball season progressed, however, the Henry High girls got to know the North High girls and discovered that they're actually okay people. "Once they [North High girls] joined our team and we got to know them, we saw that they're pretty nice." "They're even good volleyball players," another Henry High girl said. Something else happened too; the Henry High girls stopped referring to the North High players as *them* and began using the all-inclusive *us* to refer to all players on the team. Not coincidentally, that was right around the same time the North High girls ceased to be "b-----s who suck at volleyball" and became "friends who are pretty good at volleyball." Magically, the divisions between the North and Henry High volleyball players crumbled when the groups actually spent time together in pursuit of a common goal. These girls' story demonstrates a great truth about crosscultural contact: it is the most powerful antidote to divisions.

The Power of Crosscultural Contact

Gordon Allport, an early groups theorist, is said to have used the following conversation to show how much group segregation leads to bad attitudes toward the other group.

"See that man over there?"

"Yes."

"Well, I hate him."

"But you don't even know him."

"That's why I hate him."

Allport recognized that homogeneity is never harmless and introduced *contact theory* as a way of bringing groups together in order to reduce prejudice. The idea is that if group separation causes inaccurate perceptions of other groups, negative emotions and discrimination (which I've shown in the preceding chapters), then under certain conditions, direct contact between members of different groups will reverse those inaccurate perceptions, negative emotions and discrimination. This works because crosscultural contact between the groups provides information that flies in the face of inaccurate perceptions and negative emotions that would otherwise live on. It also works by forcing individuals to see the similarities between themselves and the other group. In the end, people often find that their negative beliefs about the other group are overgeneralized and untrue.

Crosscultural contact has often been described as an exercise in error reduction. If our default perceptions and emotional responses to different cultural groups are erroneous in nature, then contact creates a context in which errors can be challenged and corrected. Without contact, our errors continue to go unchallenged and often begin to take on lives of their own. As a bonus, contact reduces the anxiety that people might have about interacting with other groups. When we have had at least one positive meaningful contact experience, we are more likely to desire crosscultural contact in the future and more likely to enjoy it when we do. As the saying goes, "Once you go black, you never go back!"

Crosscultural contact based on contact theory has worked wonders to break down stubborn divisions between Protestants and Catholics in Northern Ireland, blacks and whites in post-apartheid South Africa, and black and white students in US schools. Hundreds of studies have shown that crosscultural contact is effective in increasing positive attitudes and reducing prejudice toward different others. For example, one study showed that teachers who had previously interacted with an HIV-positive individual (adult or child) had more positive attitudes toward and were much more willing to teach a child with HIV than teachers who hadn't previously interacted with an HIV-positive individual.

Crosscultural contact works its magic by (1) requiring people to see different group members as individuals, rather than nameless, faceless members of a cultural group, and (2) creating a context in which the two different groups are encouraged to form a common identity. Much like the members of the North-Henry High Polar Bear Patriots volleyball team, individuals who engage in crosscultural contact are much more likely to see members of different cultural groups in accurate, cognitively generous ways and to expand their category of *us* to include those whom they used to consider outgroup members.

Crosscultural contact can also give us a much-needed attitude adjustment toward those who are culturally different. Recent research has demonstrated that crosscultural contact has led to more positive attitudes toward the former outgroup, more trust toward the former outgroup, more guilt and forgiveness for past deeds and atrocities, and more empathy for the former outgroup. Crosscultural contact can help us to do the seemingly impossible: treat culturally different Christians in a loving, inclusive and gracious way!

But before we get ahead of ourselves, I should mention that research on contact theory has shown that simple contact between groups does not necessarily improve attitudes toward the former outgroup. In fact, it can potentially *produce* conflict and hostility. Gordon Allport once wrote, "It has sometimes been held that merely by assembling people without regard for race, color, religion, or national origin, we can thereby destroy stereotypes and develop friendly attitudes. The case is not so simple." The one-time "unity" event organized by well-intentioned Christians is a worthy idea but probably a step in the wrong direction because such events typically allow group divisions and inaccurate attitudes to go unchallenged. We should have suspected as much; worthwhile endeavors are never easy—and church unity is no exception.

Thoughtful and intentional contact between well-prepped individuals is a key to overpowering long-standing divisions. I'll describe the elements of a well-crafted crosscultural contact situation later on in this chapter. But before we can jump into planning crosscultural interactions, we must prepare ourselves and our church groups.

A Biblical Foundation for Crosscultural Unity

Sustained crosscultural interactions are not for the faint of heart. As multiethnic church leader Mark Deymaz often says, "In a multi-ethnic ministry setting, there's a 100% chance that you will be offended by someone or offend someone." In my experience, the glorious work of reconciliation is equal parts exhilarating and excruciating.

Just last week, after months of careful planning, preparation and prayer, a small group of pastoral leaders and I hosted a large multi-ethnic ministry leadership conference. While much of the conference went well, it ended on an extremely sour note when the well-meaning keynote speaker made comments that were both oppressive and offensive to many historically subjugated people in the audience. I immediately felt sick to my stomach, and my mind and heart buzzed with questions. *How could someone so awfully and insensitively misuse his power in a Christian setting, much less at a* multiethnic *ministry conference? How did this happen in spite of our efforts to create a welcoming and encouraging conference for members of all cultural groups? Did I just waste months of my time on a lost cause?* I felt betrayed, hurt and hopeless—feelings that are often experienced by reconciliation workers.

The work of reconciliation is often excruciating because it is the work of the cross. If reconciliation work isn't painful, I'd venture to say that it isn't really reconciliation work. Reconciliation requires that we partner with equally imperfect individuals who are also clumsily scaling the crosscultural learning curve, forgive those who carelessly wrong us, repeatedly ask for forgiveness, engage in awkward and unpredictable situations and, like gluttons for punishment, keep coming back for more.

As much as I hate to admit it, I am not a superhero; I know that I will stop coming back for more if I am not sustained by a strong biblical and theological foundation for crosscultural reconciliation. I will lose my will to stay in the fight if I lose sight of the fact that by reconciling with others I am simply following in Christ's reconciling footsteps. I will lose my will to stay in the fight if I lose sight of the painful cost that Christ endured in order to reconcile himself to me. I will lose my will to stay in the fight if I lose sight of the fact that even the most seemingly ineffective reconciliation work lives on in the power of the resurrection and will one day have its intended impact. If our work is not rooted in the power of the cross, we will inevitably quit. Reality check: you're not a superhero either. You too need a solid biblical and theological foundation for crosscultural unity. And we must instill these values in the people that we lead toward crosscultural unity.

As sociologists Michael Emerson and Christian Smith have discovered, many American Christians do not believe that the pursuit of crosscultural unity is particularly relevant to the faith that is expressed in their pulpits and small group meetings. As a result, they are perfectly content with homogenous church groups. Such Christians might initially respond to an exhortation to move beyond the boundaries of what is culturally similar to them, but they will not last long in the crosshairs of difficult and complicated crosscultural situations without a strong biblical and theological foundation for crosscultural relationships to sustain them.

Pastors and leaders who wish to lead their groups into crosscultural partnerships must lay a sturdy foundation that will likely require multiple weeks of teaching, conversation and application that emphasize the importance of crosscultural unity. I'm grateful for and highly recommend the excellent books that Curtiss DeYoung, Brenda Salter McNeil and Soong-Chan Rah have written on this topic.

Addressing Our Cognitive and Emotional Biases

The biases we hold against other groups have the ability to wreak havoc on our crosscultural interactions. Before we enter into such interactions, we must do the difficult work of addressing our biases and blind spots. This requires that leaders teach on and lead discussions on the biases and blind spots outlined in earlier chapters in the context of our particular church group situation and take an honest look inward to understand how our group is contributing to crosscultural divisions. This can include but is not limited to

- addressing the factors that lead our group members to congregate with similar others and distance ourselves from dissimilar others (chapter 2)

- examining our group members' perceptions of other cultural groups in the church in search of inaccuracies (chapters 3-4)

- discussing the ways in which social identity and self-esteem motives might affect how our group members perceive other groups (chapters 5-6)

- considering how our group members perceive realistic conflicts and cultural threats and how those perceptions affect our group's attitude toward other groups (chapter 7)

- deconstructing our group's cultural influences on beliefs and practices (chapter 8)

By uncovering and addressing the issues and blind spots that prevent group members from forming positive meaningful crosscultural relationships, church groups can enter crosscultural situations with their eyes open to potential pitfalls and equipped to overcome them. In addition, four elements are needed for positive crosscultural interaction: (1) working toward a larger goal, (2) creating equal status, (3) engaging in personal interaction and (4) providing leadership. Let's look at each in turn.

Working Toward a Larger Goal

Remember the Robbers Cave study that I described in chapter 7? When placed in a competitive group situation, the seemingly normal boys quickly transformed into spiteful, hostile Rattlers and Eagles who attacked each other. Muzafer Sherif, the lead researcher on the study, found that the only way to halt the conflict between the Rattlers and Eagles and get them to start liking each other was to create a common ingroup identity that encompassed both groups. Sherif did this by creating a common goal—a goal that required both groups of boys to work together in order to accomplish it. True to form, he did this in a brilliant but ethically dubious way. One day while both groups of boys were riding a dilapidated bus up a steep hill, the bus "broke down." The camp counselors told both groups of boys to get out of the bus and push it up the rest of the hill. Not only did the eleven-year-old boys survive the incredibly dangerous task, but they also bonded. By working together on a common goal, the division between the Rattlers and Eagles weakened. This initial strategy worked well, so over the course of the next few days, Sherif created several other goals that required the whole group to work together, such as fixing the camp water pump. By the end of camp, the two groups were so friendly with each other that they insisted on traveling home on the same bus. As the Rattlers and Eagles changed from competitors to collaborators, *they* became *we* and a common ingroup identity was forged.

Common goals—goals that require that we collaborate with people outside our ingroup—can powerfully bring groups together in the real world too. For example, Greeks and Turks have a long history of conflict and mistrust. But their relationship dramatically improved in 1999 when both countries experienced major earthquakes. The two countries worked together to deal with the shared tragedy and began to bridge a significant crosscultural gulf.

Common goals have effectively broken down racial divisions in US classrooms, especially in classrooms that use a cooperative learning technique called the *jigsaw classroom approach*. In these classes all of the assigned material is divided into as many parts as there are students in the group. Each student then learns his or her part of the material and is responsible for teaching it to the rest of the group. To understand all of the assigned material, each group member must contribute his or her "piece of the puzzle" while also relying on other group members to contribute their respective pieces.

Diverse classes that use the jigsaw classroom approach have discovered that when crosscultural group members need each other in order to complete the assignment, they begin to perceive each other in cognitively generous ways. Rather than relying on mental shortcuts and making inaccurate assumptions about culturally different students, they go the extra cognitive mile to perceive them as individuals. The result is that group members grow to value the crosscultural students' unique contributions and begin to see crosscultural students as members of the inclusive *we*.

Even though the jigsaw classroom approach works to break down barriers between different cultural groups, it also creates space for cultural differences to shine. Teachers who are skilled at using the approach typically assign material in ways that play to the students' cultural strengths. For example, if a Native American student expresses special interest in and knowledge of Native American history, the teacher will assign the portion of the lesson that focuses on Native American history to that student. In this way, students can proudly maintain their cultural group identity while recognizing the unique contributions that their cultural group and other cultural groups make to the larger multicultural class group.

Church groups can and should adopt the jigsaw classroom approach when engaging in crosscultural situations. The truth is that we are a body composed of interdependent parts, each with unique, God-given abilities and perspectives. Unfortunately, even though the metaphor of the body of Christ preaches interdependence, we seem to believe that the fullness of truth is found in our culturally homogenous church groups. We are convinced that all of the wisdom and knowledge that we need to succeed as Christian organizations is located within the boundary of our cultural group. Many Christian groups are like a 5000-piece puzzle that has 5000 duplicate pieces!

This line of thinking—which is prevalent in the body of Christ—runs contrary to the interdependent identity of the body that is described in 1 Corinthians 12:14-27.

Even so the body is not made up of one part but of many.

Now if the foot should say, "Because I am not a hand, I do not belong to the body," it would not for that reason stop being part of the body. And if the ear should say, "Because I am not an eye, I do not belong to the body," it would not for that reason stop being part of the body. *If the whole body were an eye, where would the sense of hearing be? If the whole body were an ear, where would the sense of smell be?* But in fact God has placed the parts in the body, every one of them, just as he wanted them to be. If they were all one part, where would the body be? As it is, there are many parts, but one body.

The eye cannot say to the hand, "I don't need you!" And the head cannot say to the feet, "I don't need you!" On the contrary, those parts of the body that seem to be weaker are indispensable, and the parts that we think are less honorable we treat with special honor. And the parts that are unpresentable are treated with special modesty, while our presentable parts need no special treatment. But God has put the body together, giving greater honor to the parts that lacked it, so that there should be no division in the body, but that its parts should have equal concern for each other. If one part suffers, every part suffers with it; if one part is honored, every part rejoices with it.

Now you are the body of Christ, and each one of you is a part of it. (Italics mine.)

Earlier I mentioned Scot McKnight's book *A Community Called Atonement*. In the concept of atonement he shows that cultural groups in the body of Christ are ideologically dependent upon the rest of the body of Christ. The various atonement metaphors Mc-

Knight describes—offering, justification, reconciliation, redemption and ransom—typically lead to cultural division. Why? Because groups think that their particular metaphor provides the entire or most important truth about atonement and that other groups' metaphors are wrong or relatively less important.

McKnight suggests that each metaphor provides a partial truth that, when integrated with the rest of the metaphors, can lead to a more whole truth. He writes, "Atonement language includes several evocative metaphors: there is a sacrificial metaphor (offering), and a legal metaphor (justification), and an interpersonal metaphor (reconciliation), and a commercial metaphor (redemption), and a military metaphor (ransom). Each is designed to carry us . . . to the *thing*. But the metaphor is *not* the thing." Rather than clinging to one theological viewpoint on atonement as the whole truth (as the *thing*), we should value and welcome the metaphors of other groups because together, they help us to understand atonement. Each theological perspective on atonement emphasizes an important aspect of atonement. No one perspective provides the whole picture.

The metaphor of the body of Christ explicitly articulates the need to value different perspectives—to be ideologically interdependent. When we enter crosscultural situations with the belief that our cultural group is holding one piece to the puzzle, we can confidently make our contribution while also looking for and valuing the contributions that other groups make, and as a result, the barriers between *us* and *them* begin to fall down. Of course, this is most likely to occur when we intentionally create crosscultural situations that are distinctly cooperative, in which we *must* rely on the other group in order to achieve the common goal.

Examples of cooperative crosscultural projects are joint church and community projects such as an anti-sex trafficking initiative, a tutoring program or a food pantry ministry. If two groups differ significantly along ideological lines, I think it is particularly powerful and poetic for them to search high and low for one important belief that they *do* have in common and build their cooperative project around that belief.

Ultimately, the type of cooperative project doesn't really matter as long as it (1) is relatively long-term (so as to foster authentic and lasting friendships) and (2) requires that each group make unique and necessary contributions to the common goal in order to achieve success (so as to foster interdependence). Within the cooperative crosscultural situation, each cultural group can provide different resources—such as knowledge, language skills, relationship and networking pathways, financial resources and culturally specific skills and perspectives—that play to that culture's strengths. Although, don't be afraid to step outside your cultural comfort zone to take risks! Simply leaving your comfort zone (e.g., to spend significant time on the other culture's "turf") can foster interdependence because it requires that you depend on them to help you navigate an unknown situation. Besides, most good things happen outside of our comfort zones.

Here's an example of a collaborative project: a church primarily composed of white twenty-somethings might collaborate with a predominantly Hispanic church to create and maintain a community garden and mini farmer's market in a local Hispanic neighborhood. In this situation, perhaps the white church can provide labor, publicity and organic farming skills, while the Hispanic church can offer labor as well as Spanish language skills, invaluable knowledge of the culture, social landscape and history of the neighborhood, and relationships with local leaders and residents.

The combined resources of the two cultural groups create a more powerful effect than if the two groups had attempted duplicate but culturally segregated projects. In social psychology, we often use the German term *gestalt*, which means that the whole is greater than the sum of its parts. When we engage in cooperative crosscultural relationships, not only are we embodying our identity as the body of Christ, but we are also more effectively working toward our common goal. When we work together, we are greater than the sum of our parts. As I wrote in chapter 2, diverse groups are more effective groups.

Creating Equal Status

There are many instances in which beautifully interdependent crosscultural interaction goals fail because well-intentioned group members do not recognize status differences that maintain divides. I recently spoke with a woman who led a prayer group for mothers of children at a diverse public school that bordered two very different neighborhoods and served both upper-middle-class white families and working-class Hispanic families. The group of women met each week on Thursday mornings at ten o'clock at a home in the predominantly white, upper-middle-class neighborhood. Even though the school was almost 50 percent Hispanic, the praying mothers realized that their group was exclusively white. Not wanting to exclude the Hispanic mothers, the women in the group reached out to them by sending them fliers and even contacting local Hispanic churches to tell them about the prayer group. Then the white women in the group waited for the Hispanic women to start attending their Thursday morning meeting.

The white women waited and waited but not one Hispanic woman ever came. The leader of the group contacted me, disappointed that their efforts had failed and searching for advice. I was encouraged by her sincere desire for crosscultural unity and asked her to consider the status differences between upper-middle-class white women and working-class Hispanic women that might impact whether or not a woman could attend a Thursday mid-morning meeting that inconveniently met outside of her neighborhood.

The leader thought about my question and concluded that even though she and her white upper-middle-class friends had the privilege of being stay-at-home moms or having flexible work schedules, perhaps the working-class Hispanic women did not. She also concluded that perhaps the two groups had differing access to convenient transportation. She began to realize that the wealthy white women perhaps needed to recognize their privilege and forfeit it in order to achieve true unity.

In pursuit of this goal, the leader befriended one of the Hispanic mothers at the school and, in getting to know her, found that she too was passionate about praying for her children. Together, they now colead a prayer meeting for both white and Hispanic moms at the home of one of the Hispanic moms on Thursdays at 9:30 p.m. The white mothers had to arrange for childcare in order to meet late at night, but they rightly considered it a small price to pay for crosscultural unity. Once they changed the time and location to one that afforded both groups equal access, the crosscultural group thrived.

Positive crosscultural interactions only work if both groups enjoy equal status. Here's the thing: not all divisions are created equal. Some divisions occur between two equal-status groups that simply disagree on an issue they deem important. However, other divisions (e.g., divisions across racial, gender or class lines) occur between groups that do not share equal status. In fact, in many cases, the divisions are the result of the higher-status group systemically oppressing the lower-status group.

For example, many traditional African American churches are segregated from "mainstream," predominantly white evangelical churches because for many years (and continuing today) white evangelical church people have explicitly and implicitly oppressed African Americans and in doing so have perpetuated status differences between blacks and whites that have given rise to racial divisions in the church. The segregated black church is an outcome of centuries of ongoing oppression from higher-status Christians, namely white Christians. In order to achieve true unity between blacks and whites, the status differences and historical and ongoing oppression must be addressed and reversed.

Miroslav Volf argues that both reconciliation and justice must go hand in hand; without one, you cannot have the other. Before two groups can enjoy renewed, healthy friendship, past wrongs must be made right through repentance, forgiveness and the return of stolen commodities (such as power, land, status, money). This might be the most difficult element to successfully pull off because it requires that both groups (*especially* the higher-status group) recognize any power or status differences that exist between them, repent for them and make a unified, concerted effort to erase them in the context of the crosscultural situation and beyond.

This is a tall order that requires a real and fierce conversation on the elephant in the church: privilege and power differentials. For some reason, high-status people (in my experience, particularly white men) have a hard time seeing and admitting that they are in fact high-status people who enjoy privileges that aren't afforded to lower-status people. Even more troubling, I've found that many white male pastors and seminary students have an even harder time admitting that these privilege and power issues exist in the church and are even perpetuated by the church. This ignorance of power and privilege differentials shows up in questions like, "Why don't more people of color come to *our* church?" The entitled sentiment behind this question is antithetical to Christ's crosscultural, privilege-abdicating example in the incarnation. Privileged people who truly understand their privilege will jump at the chance to give up their privilege by going to the other's church, in *their* cultural comfort zone, on *their* turf and on *their* terms. Quite simply, this is what unity in our upside-down kingdom often requires.

Addressing power and privilege differentials often involves rejecting powerful societal norms that support status differences. It also often involves the higher-status group's voluntarily abdicating its higher status. These are both difficult and potentially painful processes that require individuals to closely examine the ways in which their social identities (such as race, gender, economic status, education level) influence the status, power, privilege and mobility that society affords them.

Group exercises such as Peggy McIntosh's "The Invisible Knapsack," which is easily found on the web, can help to jumpstart this process. My friend Matt is a white male pastor who leads a predominantly white church that is intentionally becoming more multiethnic. He understands the importance of equal status between cultural groups in the church and thus requires that his leaders undergo extensive white-privilege education before engaging in any ministry leadership, much less multiethnic ministry leadership. He's got the right idea.

Once status differences between the groups are addressed (at the very least in the context of the crosscultural situation), groups must work hard to ensure that equal status is maintained. Since status differences in the larger society likely remain intact, these differences can easily "spill over" into the crosscultural situation. Research suggests that even among well-intentioned groups, the dominant cultural group in a particular society can easily dominate a supposedly crosscultural situation.

Ifat Moaz found that in structured, crosscultural encounters between Jewish and Palestinian teachers, members of the dominant group tended to control the cooperative task. Even though all involved were interested in giving everyone equal status, the high-status people fell into old patterns of domination and oppression. This happens all of the time in the American church; dominant group members make an effort to be inclusive of diverse cultural groups, but their lack of knowledge about status and power leads them to subtly or blatantly perpetuate divisions.

Many people of color who attend predominantly white churches and Christian colleges and seminaries talk about feeling explicitly welcomed by the majority group but implicitly excluded and disempowered. On the surface (and for the most part), members of the well-intentioned white majority are *really, really* nice to them. People of color are greeted warmly in the hallways, on the bike path and in the pews. They are explicitly told that they are welcome at the church or school. They are even invited into the homes of colleagues, classmates and fellow church members. However, despite these welcoming individual actions, people of color often report that their experience at these Christian organizations is marked by feelings of disempowerment, loneliness, marginalization, exclusion and misunderstanding. This response both befuddles and discourages the well-intentioned white people and leads people of color to experience a seemingly unshakeable feeling of what Volf calls "psychological homelessness." They feel out of place, on the edge of the circle, disconnected from the life-giving heartbeat of the community.

Unfortunately, the well-intentioned but uninformed efforts of the majority group rarely work. When talking about diversity and reconciliation in the church, American Christians (who tend to be highly individualistic) often focus on the explicit actions that individuals can take to make different others feel welcome. However, a focus on *explicit, individual* actions can easily lead people in the majority group to ignore the *implicit, collective* actions that communicate to people of color that they are not at all welcome and they are not equal members of the group. Even though these actions often go unnoticed by the majority group, they ring loud and clear to people of color, like a noisy alarm that won't turn off.

Nancy Schlossburg introduced the concepts of *mattering* and *marginality* to talk about the subtle but powerful ways in which a group of people can include or exclude and empower and disempower different others. Mattering and marginality exist on opposite ends of a continuum, such that the more an individual feels like she matters and is empowered, the less she feels marginalized and disempowered, and vice versa.

Individuals tend to feel like they matter when their experience in an organization is marked by the *presence* of all of the factors in figure 9.1; they tend to feel marginalized when their experience in an organization is marked by the *absence* of one or more of the factors.

Figure 9.1.

Identification	Feeling that other people will be proud of your accomplishments or saddened by your failures
Attention	Feeling that you command the sincere attention or interest of people in the group
Importance	Believing that another person cares about what you want, think and do, or is concerned about your fate
Appreciation	A feeling of being highly regarded and acknowledged by others
Dependence	Feeling integrated in the community such that your behaviors/actions are based on how others depend on you

For example, the vast majority of the students in my introductory psychology course are eighteen-year-old, first-year students. In order to teach well to this specific group, I use lots of examples that resonate in their teenage world. However, two nontraditional students, both over fifty years old, recently joined the class. I was ecstatic to have more age diversity in the class, and I explicitly welcomed the two older students. But I continued to use only teenage examples in class and pose class discussion questions that related more to a teenage world. Of course, my eighteen-year-old students were perfectly content; the class catered to their concerns, needs and experiences. But by the third week of the semester, each of the older students approached me separately and told me that they felt "out of place," disempowered and disconnected in class. Uh-oh! I had meant well and had explicitly *told* the older students that they were welcomed, empowered and important members of the class. And then I implicitly *showed* them that they weren't by powerfully contributing to a class culture that only gave voice to the dominant group. Actions speak louder than words.

Similarly, I've witnessed plenty of so-called unity events in the body of Christ that are so heavily influenced by white culture that any other collaborating cultures are rendered invisible. This typically happens when the majority culture takes an "our way or the highway" approach and requires the minority culture to assimilate to the majority culture. This can be unintentional but it has grave consequences, not only because it is oppressive but also because it leaves no room for much-needed diverse cultural expression. We dishonor the image of God in diverse people when we require them to assimilate to the dominant culture in our church, organization or event.

If issues of status, privilege and power are not effectively addressed within the crosscultural situation, existing divisions will deepen and widen. A good amount of research suggests that diversity has negative consequences, particularly when minority group members do not have equal status with other group members and do not feel that they are valued members of the group. When this is the case, crosscultural groups often perform worse than homogenous groups, especially when the group work requires that group members depend on each other's skills and performance. In addition, crosscultural group members tend to communicate with each other less and react to each other with more emotional negativity.

Perhaps the most troubling finding is that while cultural diversity might be uncomfortable for all group members, low-status minorities often bear the brunt of the discomfort; they are less satisfied with the group, experience less psychological closeness to the organization, perceive less supervisor support and experience less procedural justice within the organization. These experiences defeat the purpose of unity-building crosscultural interactions! To put it bluntly, if you're not willing to do the uncomfortable work of addressing and eradicating power and privilege differences in the church and beyond, you shouldn't bother with unity and reconciliation. You can't have the latter without the former. Like I said, reconciliation is not for the faint of heart.

We must address how power and status differentials are perpetuated by both individuals and the group culture. In this case, a commitment to equal status often means going against societal norms by refusing to allow the dominant cultural group to dominate the crosscultural situation and intentionally giving the historically subjugated group the power and resources to exert influence.

Engaging in Personal Interaction

Homogeneity—*not* personally interacting with people outside of our cultural group—directly causes many of the divisions and wrong perceptions that I've discussed in this book. For this reason, no crosscultural interaction would be complete without fostering authentic, lasting crosscultural relationships. When we get to know culturally different people on a personal level, our wrong beliefs about them are challenged, especially if their behaviors clearly negate the group stereotype. Remember the moms' Bible study that I joined at my church? Once I got to know the women on a personal level, I realized that my stereotypes of the group (e.g., that they despise me, that they are all complementarian, that they are obsessed with their kids and can't have meaningful conversations about anything other than the color and consistency of their kid's poop) were simply untrue. But without that personal interaction, my stereotypes would have lived on in my mind, growing more ridiculous over time (as if they weren't already ridiculous enough). Once we get to know people on an interpersonal level, we cease to view them solely as nondescript group members and begin to see them as individuals. In turn, this undermines many of the negative perceptions that we once held for that group. Personal interaction sets us free from our false perceptions of *them*.

Research on crosscultural relationships between Catholics and Protestants in Northern Ireland has found that prior to crosscultural contact, both groups tended to associate uniquely human attributes (e.g., intelligence and the ability to experience secondary emotions such as guilt and shame) to their ingroup, but not to the outgroup (a process social psychologists call *infrahumanization*). Catholics believed that Protestants were less capable of feeling guilt and shame and by extension were less *human* (like how many of us would perceive a psychopath). And Protestants believed the same about Catholics. But once Catholic and Protestant groups engaged in crosscultural cooperative projects and began to get to know each other on a personal level, their negative perceptions of the other group were disconfirmed and they no longer believed that the other group members were basically psychopaths.

Perhaps the most important reason why personal interaction is so valuable in a crosscultural situation is that it motivates us to see other group members as individuals and provides a natural, ongoing setting in which we can develop friendships. Remember at the end of chapter 3 when I mentioned that if we are motivated to override automatic and false perceptions, we can do it by choosing to be cognitively generous (rather than sticking to our normal cognitive miserliness) as we perceive culturally different people? Well, personal interaction, especially when we are working on a collaborative project, can be just the kick in the pants that we need to be cognitively generous.

Think about it: If you're working one-on-one with a person and you are relying on her to help you complete a project that you both value, it's in your best interest to view her as accurately as possible. If you go the cognitive miser route, painting broad strokes of her group and judging her solely on what you think you know about the group, you risk offending her, and in doing so, jeopardize the project. It makes much more sense to exert the extra energy needed to perceive her in cognitively generous ways—by correcting inaccurate beliefs and seeking individual information about her. It's good for your relationship with her, good for the collaborative goal and, last but certainly not least, the right thing to do.

When we cooperate with culturally different others on a personal level, we're more likely to present ourselves in friendly and ingratiating ways, which makes us more likable to them and increases the likelihood that they will actually want to be our friends.

Leadership

When it comes to crosscultural unity, leadership is vital. Pastors and other leaders *must* lead the charge in building crosscultural bridges. The last element needed for positive crosscultural interactions is the people of power to repeatedly talk about the importance of crosscultural contact and put their money where their mouth is by allocating resources in support of crosscultural contact.

One way leaders can do this is by modeling crosscultural unity for other group members. Long ago, Pettigrew argued that group leaders should model contact for other group members. More recent research on the *extended-contact hypothesis* supports this argument. The extended-contact hypothesis says that people who are friends with people who are friends with outgroup members are more likely to have positive attitudes toward the outgroup. In other words, pastors and leaders can begin to break down barriers between their respective cultural groups by simply modeling crosscultural relationships for their congregants to see. When a church member sees his or her leader engaged in a crosscultural friendship, the church member will be more likely to follow suit. Of course this requires that the leader address his or her own biases and impediments to unity first.

I recently spoke with a white organizational leader who was discouraged that the kids who participated in his racially diverse after-school program were only playing with kids of their same race. He had made several attempts to encourage them to interact crossculturally, but nothing seemed to work. After listening to his description of the program, I asked him whether the adult leadership team was as diverse as the young participants and whether the leadership team modeled crosscultural friendships for the kids. Before he could answer no to both questions, he knew what he needed to do. Research on the extended-contact hypothesis stresses the importance of leader-to-leader crosscultural friendships—not only for the sake of leader-to-leader unity, but also for the sake of culture-to-culture unity.

But leadership by example can only take us so far. Leaders must take more active steps toward crosscultural unity by clearly defining the norms in favor of crosscultural unity. If authority figures set norms and regulations in place that favor crosscultural contact (such as the famous *Brown v. Board of Education of Topeka* US Supreme Court decision), groups will be much more likely to conform to them. Conversely, norms that favor cultural divisions have been shown to minimize the positive impact of crosscultural contact in places like South Africa and Northern Ireland.

Pastors and church leaders must lead by defining and communicating norms in their church groups that clearly support crosscultural unity and encourage group members to bravely venture outside of their cultural comfort zones in pursuit of unity. This can include but is not limited to

- modifying the organizational purpose to include unity goals
- teaching/preaching regularly on the topic of unity
- allocating significant organizational resources toward the goal of unity
- addressing and correcting structural inequities in the church/organization culture
- offering seminars to equip congregants for crosscultural unity
- developing multicultural leadership
- regularly inviting different cultural voices to speak in the pulpit and elsewhere

Church leaders can lead in the crosscultural situation by ensuring that the challenging goal of maintaining equal status is achieved. Leaders can do this is by closely moderating crosscultural discussions. Group members who hail from low-status groups in society are much less likely to express their opinions in crosscultural settings. However, group members who hail from higher-status groups often dominate the discussion, even if the information they possess is not more valid or useful.

Since group leaders have high status in the group, they can effectively solicit information from all group members by setting a group norm that all members should feel free to speak up because each group member can offer unique and valuable information and by specifically supporting opinions from low-status group members. In this way, group leaders can be arbiters of justice who confer status on those who need it and ensure that all participants have an equal place at the table. However, this means that group leaders must be aware of their own power in the situation, as well as the subtle (even invisible to those who are in power) ways in which the organizational culture effectively silences low-status group members, even as they are explicitly asked to contribute to group discussions. In many ways, the church is a justice desert. High-status leaders can change that.

Christians who are empowered by an awareness of the automatic cognitive and emotional contributors to cultural divisions and who have experienced positive crosscultural contact can begin to overcome the divisions by building meaningful relationships with different others. While initially fraught with distance, distrust and misperceptions, these relationships can come to be characterized by empathy, a willingness to ask for and grant forgiveness, positive attitudes toward the former outgroup, willingness to learn from former outgroup members and inclusion of former outgroup members into the group. Only then can the church be one.

Chapter 9 Questions

1. Can you think of an example of how collaborative projects have built crosscultural bridges in your community?

2. How might a strong biblical foundation for crosscultural unity help you as you engage with different cultures?

3. I encourage you to complete the "Invisible Knapsack" exercise. How did you feel while you were doing it? What were you thinking?

4. In what ways are you a privileged/powerful person in your community?

5. In what ways do you lack privilege or power in your community?

6. Think about the difference between mattering and marginality. Do you think that you matter in your church community? If not, why not? What do you think will help?

7. Consider the many cultural groups within a church (e.g., race, gender, class, education, politics, marital status, etc.). Who are the nonmajority/lower-status members in your church?

8. Do nonmajority members in your church community feel like they matter? What are some subtle and blatant ways that your church culture marginalizes nonmajority members. What can you do as a leader? What can the church do?

9. Think of another cultural group with whom you'd like to build a bridge. How might your level of privilege differ from that of someone in that culture?

10. What would it look like for you to create a crosscultural space in which both groups have equal status? What would you have to give up? What would you have to gain?

11. How do you as a leader plan to lead others into crosscultural unity?

10

The Preeminence
of (Identity in) Christ

How Things Can and Should Be

As you probably remember, I have a love/hate relationship with the city of Chicago. The city is beautiful and diverse but also astoundingly segregated. As we've seen, the current depressing reality is that Christians often act as if the kingdom of God is supposed to look like Chicago. In theory, we support the vision of a diverse, integrated and interdependent body of Christ, but we sure as heck don't want to venture outside of our homogenous churches to live the vision.

But there's hope! Things don't have to stay the same. Ideally, this book has helped you to understand why it's so difficult for Christians to break out of the pattern of homogenous churches and antagonism toward culturally different others. And hopefully, this book has also helped you understand that the primary problem is that our identities are too small. We tend to rely most on our smaller, cultural identities and ignore our larger, common identity as members of the body of Christ. The tips that I've given at the end of each chapter—for example, using the inclusive "we" to describe other cultural groups in the church (chapter 3) or affirming our identities as members of the body of Christ (chapter 6)—as well as the guidelines for facilitating crosscultural interactions (chapter 9) are aimed at helping us to relativize our smaller identities and adopt a common identity as the larger body of Christ. Indeed, adopting a common identity is the key to tearing down cultural divisions and working toward reconciliation.

Why Does a Common Identity Matter?

The amount of effort required to change the way we think about ourselves and adopt a new, common identity is significant but well worth it. Research shows that many of the categorizing, self-esteem and cultural threat processes that wreak divisive havoc on the church (that I described in chapters 3-8) are reversed when we finally stop thinking of ourselves as *us* versus *them* and begin to think of ourselves as one large ingroup.

Lowell Gaertner, Jack Dovidio and colleagues have introduced the common ingroup identity model: "If members of different groups are induced to conceive of themselves as a single group rather than as two completely separate groups, attitudes toward former outgroup members will become more positive through the cognitive and motivational forces that result from ingroup formation—a consequence that could increase the sense of connectedness across group lines." If we begin to see outgroup members as ingroup members, we will begin to treat them like ingroup members, which is generally pretty good. Ultimately, when we come together, we will not see each other as threatening competitors, but as diverse fellow group members.

In fact, many research studies show that a common identity is invaluable in breaking down barriers in crosscultural situations. Here are a few of the good things that happen when we loosen our grip on smaller cultural identities in favor of adopting a common identity as the body of Christ.

When they become we, we naturally like them a whole lot more.

In one study, Gaertner, Dovidio and colleagues surveyed African American, Chinese, Caucasian, Hispanic, Japanese, Jewish, Korean and Vietnamese students at a multiethnic high school. They found that students who perceived the student body as "one group" or as "different groups playing on the same team" (an example of a dual identity, which I'll talk about later) were much more likely to express positive feelings toward other ethnic groups than students who viewed the student body as comprising distinct groups.

Another study found that British college students liked French college students more when their European identity was more powerful than their British identity. However, British students rather disliked French students when their identity as Brits trumped their identity as Europeans.

When our common identity becomes more important to us than our smaller cultural identities, former outgroup members become fellow ingroup members—they are treated like one of *us* and we instinctively like them.

Plus, when we know that *they* have also adopted an identity that includes us, we like them more. We love it when other people include us in their group because it implicitly tells us that they want to associate with us. This simple act prevents inaccurate metaperceptions ("what we think they think of us," discussed in chapter 3) from forming or continuing. When we no longer think of ourselves as *us* versus *them*, we are no longer convinced that *they* don't like us and don't want to interact with us.

When they *become* we, *we're more open to receiving helpful criticism from them.* In chapter 3, we saw how simple categorizing often prevents us from receiving much-needed help from other cultural groups in the body of Christ. In chapter 7, we saw how other processes such as need for cognitive closure also prevent us from receiving much-needed input from other Christian groups. These tendencies not only powerfully drive groups apart but also prevent them from collaborating when it is most desperately needed.

A common identity can override these tendencies and help group members to receive valuable information from other cultural groups. Wendi Gardner and colleagues suggest that when we adopt a common identity, we expand our sense of self to include culturally different people and, in doing so, are no longer threatened by their achievements, performance or perspective. When we see *them* as fellow group members, we begin to view *their* resources as *our* resources and are happy to receive them, even if that means accepting constructive criticism that temporarily stings.

Case in point: By the mid-1990s, the once-strong Bethlehem Lutheran Church in Minneapolis was experiencing the effects of the urban decline that was sweeping across America. Enticed by suburban life, over 1,000 Bethlehem attendees had moved out of the city limits and begun attending suburban churches. The church leaders were in dire straits; not willing to go down without a fight, they began looking for help.

They found it in an unexpected place: among Southern Baptists. Admittedly, the church leaders were skeptical when they heard of the Purpose-Driven Church conference at Saddleback Church in Southern California. They grumbled to themselves, *What? Lutherans learn from Southern Baptists? Not likely.* There was real hesitancy on the part of the staff and elder board, but they ultimately felt the Holy Spirit prompting them to attend the conference.

According to lead pastor Christopher Nelson, their foray into the Southern Baptist world did not begin well. During the first session of the conference, Pastor Nelson and the other leaders found themselves distracted by their sharp disagreement with Pastor Rick Warren's theology. However, during the first coffee break, the Bethlehem team got together and made a conscious collective decision to loosen their grip on their cultural group identity (Lutheran) and adopt a humble stance. "We had to lay down our Lutheran biases. We knew that if we insisted on fighting with him [Pastor Warren] over what's theologically correct, we were going to miss everything that we came out there for," Pastor Nelson says. The leadership team returned to Minnesota armed with a new approach for doing urban church and a teaching style that was not only biblically and theologically sound and relevant to the congregation (as it was prior to attending the conference), but also application oriented and directed toward life change. Since then, the church attendance has rebounded, giving has more than tripled and the church is now making a strong impact, with people serving in the community and across the world.

As the trailblazing pastor of the first mainline church to adopt the Purpose-Driven Church model, Pastor Nelson has learned the importance of adopting a common identity in order to learn from and teach each other. "Rick Warren calls me his 'liberal Christian friend' and I call him 'my conservative Christian friend.' We've had some interesting political conversations, but we don't have to agree on everything. . . . He says some things that make my skin crawl, but so did Martin Luther."

Even though his church retains its distinct Lutheran identity (Pastor Nelson says the church remains "as Lutheran and liturgical as the day is long"), its new common identity now includes Southern Baptists. In fact, Pastor Nelson now teaches the Purpose-Driven Church model to Lutheran churches as far away as India, saying, "Evangelicals really know how to communicate and know how to do church, so someone tell me what is wrong with that? Why can't we learn from that?"

Indeed, when we adopt a common identity, we are more likely to see how other groups can help us and are more willing to receive constructive criticism from them. Matthew Hornsey and colleagues found that Anglo Australian (ingroup) participants were more likely to receive constructive criticism from Asian Australians (outgroup) when Asian Australians were thought of as fellow members of a shared identity (that is, Australians). Much like Pastor Nelson and the rest of the Bethlehem Lutheran leadership team, the Anglo

Australians found that when the outgroup becomes a friend rather than a foe, defensiveness is no longer necessary.

When they *become we, we forgive them more easily and are less likely to expect them to experience collective guilt.* When different cultural groups attempt to reconcile, they must first confront the past wrongs that one or both groups committed. In the last chapter, I talked about how high-status group members must acknowledge and repent for any role that they have played in oppressing lower-status groups. But low-status group members also have an important role to play—namely, they must do the difficult work of forgiving. Forgiveness is crucial to healthy crosscultural interaction; before true relationship can begin, forgiveness must occur. Research shows that crosscultural situations that lack forgiveness are dominated by hostility, vengefulness and increased rumination about past wrongs. But we all know forgiveness is difficult to come by.

South African archbishop Desmond Tutu insists that for forgiveness to occur, both victims and perpetrators must adopt a single, common identity. Research supports this idea by showing that a common identity fuels forgiveness by helping victimized group members to distinguish between current members of a high-status group and their guilty ancestors. When we adopt a common identity that includes *them*, we are less likely to lump them together with past members of their group who caused the offense(s).

Michael Wohl and Nyla Branscombe tested this idea with Jewish participants. They hypothesized that Jewish participants who adopted a common identity when reflecting on the Holocaust would be less likely to associate contemporary Germans with past Germans and more likely to forgive them for the past than if the Jewish participants remained solely rooted in their cultural identity.

To test this, the researchers used a common identity (that is, human identity) by asking participants to reflect on the Holocaust as an event in which humans did horrible things to other humans. They found that when participants perceived the Holocaust in this way, they were less likely to associate contemporary Germans with Holocaust-era Germans and more likely to express interest in forgiveness. However, when participants perceived the Holocaust as an event in which members of the outgroup (Germans) committed atrocities against members of the ingroup (Jews), they were more likely to hold contemporary Germans responsible for the Holocaust and less likely to express interest in forgiveness.

In another study, Wohl and Branscombe looked at the relationship between Native Canadians and white Canadians. Similar to the United States, Native lands were confiscated by white Canadians in the nineteenth century through a series of lopsided treaties. Also much like the United States, the effects of this historical injustice remain palpable. The average Native Canadian's income is two-thirds that of the average white Canadian; less than 50 percent of Native Canadian homes have basic amenities such as sewer and water connections; and 60 percent of Native Canadians live below the poverty line. Further, Native Canadians suffer from society-wide discrimination that results in lower levels of employment and · less managerial and professional job opportunities compared to white Canadians. Clearly, Native Canadians continue to experience similar troubles to the ones that began when white Canadians stole their land from them.

To test whether adopting a common identity helps to facilitate forgiveness for *current* wrongdoing, Wohl and Branscombe repeated the Jewish Holocaust study with Native Canadians, asking Native Canadians to reflect on the current and past treatment of Natives in Canada. The results mirrored those of the Jewish Holocaust study: when Native Canadians adopted a common identity that included white Canadians, they were more likely to perceive the wrongdoing that white Canadians committed as consistent with the harm that many groups have committed against each other throughout global history. As a result, Native Canadians expressed greater interest in forgiveness.

Forgiveness is an essential building block for crosscultural relationships, and new, larger identities pave the way for it.

When they *become* we, *our diversity initiatives will finally begin to work.* As I showed in chapter 2, in many ways diverse groups are more effective groups. Specifically, diverse groups are more creative and generate more feasible and effective ideas. However, this is only the case if all group members feel heard and appreciated.

Here's the thing. I rarely come across Christian organizations that truly want diversity. Oh, everyone says they want diversity, and some organizations even go through all of the pomp and circumstance of launching expensive diversity initiatives from time to time. But really, what many people want is a group of happy minorities who will happily pose for media publications and happily assimilate to the dominant culture without so much as a peep. Everyone wants diversity, but no one wants to actually be diverse.

Unfortunately, this happens because even Christian groups who hope to attract more diverse members continue to idolize their smaller cultural identity. Churches and Christian organizations want participants from diverse cultures but they are too obsessed with their own culture to allow diverse people to influence it. Rather, they require diverse people to assimilate to and bow down to the dominant culture, just as the majority group has done. Diverse participants who make any attempt to exert diverse cultural influence are silenced and shunned. *How dare they try to change our perfect little utopian culture?* we ask ourselves. *How dare they?*

When we idolize our cultural group identity, giving it higher priority than our common group identity, minority group members are not truly invited to participate in the organization as valuable members of the all-inclusive *we*. Rather, they are invited to participate in the organization as *them*—subordinate outgroup members and second-class citizens. Until we relativize our smaller cultural identities and adopt a common ingroup identity, our diversity initiatives are doomed to failure because we will never fully appreciate our diverse brothers and sisters and they will not feel appreciated.

A sports psychologist named George Cunningham studied teams of ethnically diverse track and field coaches and found that a common ingroup identity made all the difference in increasing group members' appreciation for their ethnically dissimilar colleagues. When coaches identified with the team more than they identified with their ethnicity, they were more appreciative of the ethnic diversity among the other coaches and more likely to be satisfied with their fellow coaches. Further, when all coaches adopted a common ingroup identity, ethnic minority coaches felt valued and expressed more positive work experiences. However, when none of the coaches adopted a common ingroup identity, the disadvantages of diversity were striking: strife, poor performance and dissatisfaction.

When we all adopt a common ingroup identity, we invite dissimilar others to participate in the group as first-class group members who have the same rights and power that all other group members possess. Further, we perceive ethnically dissimilar persons as ingroup members who offer valuable insights and perspective. With a common ingroup identity, our diversity initiatives start out on solid footing.

When **they** *become* **we,** *we treat each other better.* As I've discussed in previous chapters, many forces in society create barriers between groups. As a result, many of us think it's perfectly normal to interact with ingroup members in relatively positive ways and interact with outgroup members in less positive ways. No one seems bothered when we make snarky comments about other Christian groups or fail to help them; it all seems very natural. However, Christian groups who hope to positively change the status quo and begin treating other groups well will find that a common identity is particularly useful.

In an experimental field study, the researchers predicted that university affiliation (the common identity) would trump race (ingroup/outgroup distinctions) at a college football game. Depending on the experimental condition, white game attendees were approached by either white interviewers from the same university (made apparent by a baseball cap with the university's logo), white interviewers from the opposing university (made apparent by a baseball cap with the opposing university's logo), black interviewers from the same university or black interviewers from the opposing university. All participants were asked to volunteer a few minutes of time to complete a brief survey.

The researchers found that whites were willing to help white interviewers by completing the survey regardless of university affiliation. This was expected; race trumped university affiliation as whites categorized all whites as ingroup members, even when they were apparently rooting for the opposing team. However, whites were far more likely to help black interviewers when they shared a university affiliation with them, compared to black interviewers who represented the opposing team. This research shows that a common identity can overcome powerful social divisions and encourage individuals to help those that they otherwise would not have helped. By simply expanding our ingroup category to include *them*, we begin to treat the *them* better.

Plus, research shows that when we categorize a person as an ingroup member rather than as an outgroup member we like them more, believe that we share more beliefs and values with them, remember more positive things about them and are less inclined to blame them for accidents or negative events. If we are working with a common identity, many of the categorizing processes that were once detrimental to crosscultural relations are neutralized.

Should We All Be Colorblind?

I often come across churches and organizations that are diverse in composition but not in expression. A census-like survey of the group would suggest that many different cultures are represented, but interaction with the group suggests that only one culture is given voice. All other cultures have assimilated to the dominant cultural expression.

These groups have succumbed to colorblindness—or more generally, culture-blindness. The idea of a common ingroup identity that trumps all subordinate identities might seem to suggest that we should all relinquish our cultural identities and ignore our cultural differences. However, to do this would violate the metaphor of the body of Christ, in which each group expresses its unique perspective and function in coordination with other groups and in submission to the head, Jesus Christ.

Volf partially defines exclusion as erasing or ignoring distinctions. When we don't recognize the differences, the uniqueness in other individuals or groups, we can't be interdependent. It means they have no significant resources, talents or experiences to offer us that we do not already have. In essence, "the other then emerges as an inferior being who must either be assimilated by being made like" us or subjugated to us. Culture-blindness is simply disunity disguised; it falls short of the unity to which we have been called.

Gaertner and Dovidio are quick to point out that adopting a common identity does not mean that one must completely forsake one's smaller cultural identity. Anyone who watches football knows that offensive and defensive squads on a football team can operate as two distinct groups that work together in the context of a common identity.

To reject important subordinate group distinctions (such as cultural differences) and engage in colorblindness is to lose important information about individuals and their distinct cultures. For example, research on colorblind policies in integrated schools shows that teachers in these schools tend not to notice when students self-segregate, tend not to notice justice issues such as racial differences in student suspension rates and fail to incorporate teaching materials that represent the diversity of the students. It seems that

colorblindness is not the answer. Rather than completely rejecting
smaller cultural identities, Gaertner and Dovidio suggest that individuals maintain *dual identities*—identifying with a smaller cultural group within the context of a common group.

To show that this is possible, Gaertner and colleagues conducted
a study in which participants were placed in groups with either
fellow Republicans or fellow Democrats. Each group was asked to
complete a task with their politically like-minded group members.
Once they completed the task, they were asked to complete a
second task in which they had to prioritize a list of measures to
reduce the government's budget deficit and were told that each
group member would receive ten dollars if they successfully completed the task.

Some of the politically segregated groups were allowed to
remain segregated and intact for the second task. However, some
of the groups were required to collaborate with a group composed
of their political rivals. In this way, researchers created larger combined groups that included one group of Republicans and one
group of Democrats. After the second budget-deficit task was completed, participants were questioned about their perceptions of the
two groups (Republicans and Democrats) and of the members of
the two groups.

Gaertner and his colleagues found that participants who had
worked with both like-minded and opposing group members liked
and valued the opposing group and its members more. But they
found that this only happened when the participants perceived the
combined group membership as two subgroups (Republicans and
Democrats) within the common group (the budget-deficit task
group) and maintained their specific political identity as they adopted a common group identity. However, participants who did
not perceive two subgroups with the group did not like and value
the opposing group and its members.

The researchers concluded that adopting a dual identity helped combined group participants to recognize that each political group brought uniquely valuable expertise to the table, thus paving the way for positive perceptions of the opposing political group. In this way, a dual identity enables group members to perceive each other in more positive ways.

Indeed, racial bias researcher Jennifer Richeson has found that those who adopt a multicultural perspective—in which group differences are not only acknowledged, but also celebrated—exhibit less racial bias than those who adopt a colorblind perspective. When you maintain a dual identity and are in the habit of acknowledging and celebrating difference, you're more likely to perceive difference in a positive manner. Further, cognition research suggests that when group members possess dual identities, the two levels of categorizing are crossed and the perceived similarity of the common group (e.g., followers of Christ) overrides differences between the smaller cultural group (e.g., ethnicity), thus allowing group members to acknowledge and value difference but ultimately unite under the vast umbrella of the common group.

The Church as First Family

The act of adopting a common identity that supersedes all other identities is a daunting, even painful, one. However, research shows that it is the key to true unity. It is consistent with Jesus' teachings that the household of God is to take precedence over all other households. Rodney Clapp writes, "Jesus creates a new family. It is the new first family, a family of his followers that now demands primary allegiance. In fact, it demands allegiance even over the old first family, the biological family."

To embrace our identities in this new, common family, we must engage in the difficult process of lessening our grip on the identities that we have idolized and clung to for far too long. In many ways, this process will jar our souls, wreaking havoc on the satisfyingly homogenous existence in which are rooted. At first, it will feel painfully unnatural because we have lived outside of our true identities for so long that the truth seems wrong. I guarantee you that we will want to quit.

Gerd Theissen imagines the pain a fictional Hebrew mother might have experienced in reaction to Jesus' transforming call to join the family of God. She says, "He [Jesus] corrupts the young people. It all sounds fine: Blessed are you who weep for you will laugh. But what does he actually do? He makes parents weep over lost sons. He promises everything will change. But what actually changes? Families are destroyed because children run away from their parents." If we answer the call to adopt a common identity, our lives as we know them will be destroyed. However, once the transformation is complete, we will see its beautiful fruit and wonder how we ever lived within the confines of our homogenous groups.

Much like the apostle Peter who was shocked into a new reality when God asked him to loosen his powerful grip on his cultural values, travel a great distance to the house of "the other" and engage in unnatural fellowship with him (Acts 9–11), we too must embark on a similarly shocking journey if we are to fully experience the reality of the body of Christ.

We Know Who to Follow

Armed with an introductory understanding of why divisions exist and how to begin to overcome them, we must take the leap into the unknown in order to find the success stories that lay outside of concepts of Right Christian and Wrong Christian. We may not know exactly where we are headed or how we are going to get there, but we know who to imitate.

Jesus' willingness to cross boundaries to reconcile with others is evidenced not only in grandiose acts like dying on the cross, but also in simple, everyday acts like washing his disciples' feet. I can't imagine washing the disciples' hairy and crusty feet. But Jesus crossed the boundary of dirty feet in order to lovingly pursue his disciples. That his followers were very human and, quite frankly, a tad bit annoying at times, presented another boundary for Jesus to cross. Plus, he had to cross a major status difference between him and his followers (hence the titles "Teacher" and "followers"). Jesus crossed multiple boundaries in order to pursue his followers in humility and love.

Then Jesus did something surprising. After Jesus washed his followers' feet, you'd expect him to turn around and ask at least one of them to wash his feet. Typically, when we do something nice for someone, we expect the person to do something nice for us in return. According to this "norm of reciprocity," it would have been appropriate for Jesus to ask one of his followers to wash his feet. Also, after a long day in the dust, Jesus' feet needed a good bath. But Jesus surprised his followers by telling them to go wash other people's feet, rather than his feet. Essentially, he said, "I pursued you in humility and love. Now go and pursue others in humility and love."

Not only is Jesus serious about crossing boundaries to pursue us, but he's also equally serious about our crossing boundaries to pursue others. He has shown us how to do it.

Notes

Chapter 2

p. 24   In fact, Chicago was recently named: Bargo, M., Jr. (2012, October 2). Chicago, the new capital of segregation [Web log post]. Retrieved from http://www.americanthinker.com/2012 /10/chicago_the_new_capital_of_segregation.html

p. 24   Due to Chicago's twenty-three: US Census Bureau. (2000). Retrieved from http://www.census.gov/

p. 25   "People who view themselves as extroverted": Bergen, K. (2009, October 26). Personality maps characterize Chicagoans: Extroverted and agreeable people to the south, experimental and neurotic types to the north. *Chicago Tribune.* Retrieved from http://articles.chicagotribune.com/2009-10-26/ news/0910250149_1_maps-national-data-cluster

p. 25   However, the Windy City's: Biles, R. (2001). Race and housing in Chicago. *Journal of the Illinois State Historical Society, 94,* 31-38.

p. 26   Political scientists Naomi Cahn and June Carbone: Cahn, N., & Carbone, J. (2010). *Red families v. blue families: Legal polarization and the creation of culture.* New York: Oxford University Press.

p. 26   "Burger King Christianity": Raschke, C. (2008). *The next reformation: Why evangelicals must embrace postmodernity.* Grand Rapids: Baker Academic, p. 162.

p. 28   As Cahn and Carbone have noted: Cahn & Carbone, *Red families v. blue families.*

p. 28   Indeed, sociologists Michael Emerson and Christian Smith point out: Emerson, M., & Smith, C. (2000). *Divided by faith: Evangelical religion and the problem of race in America.* New York: Oxford University Press.

p. 28   Further, theologian Scot McKnight suggests: McKnight, S. (2007). *A community called atonement.* Nashville: Abingdon.

p. 28   "At 11 a.m. Sunday morning": King, M. L., Jr. (1963). As cited in Hall, D., Matz, D., & Wood, W. (2010). Why don't we practice what we preach? A meta-analytic review of religious racism. *Personality and Social Psychology Review, 14,* 126-39.

p. 28   "Contrary to popular belief": Ustinov, P. (1977). *Dear me.* New York: Penguin.

p. 29   One research study revealed: Moreland, R. L., & Beach, S. R. (1992). Exposure effects in the classroom: The development of affinity among students. *Journal of Experimental Social Psychology, 28,* 255-76.

p. 30   One classic researcher: Newcomb, T. (1961). *The acquaintance process.* New York: Holt, Rinehart and Winston.

p. 30   More recent research suggests: Macionis, J. (2003). *Society: The basics.* Englewood Cliffs, NJ: Prentice Hall; McPherson, M., Smith-Lovin, L., & Cook, J. (2001). Birds of a feather: Homophily in social networks. *Annual Review of Sociology, 27,* 415-44.

p. 30   Quite simply, we like people: Byrne, D. (1971). *The attraction paradigm.* New York: Academic Press; Byrne, D. (1997). An overview (and underview) of research and theory within the attraction paradigm. *Journal of Social and Personal Relationships, 14,* 417-31; Luo, S., & Klohnen, E. (2005). Assortative mating and marital quality in newlyweds: A couple-centered approach. *Journal of Personality and Social Psychology, 88,* 304-26.

p. 30   Research shows that "I-sharing": Pinel, E., Long, A., Landau, M., Alexander, K., & Pyszczynski, T. (2006). Seeing I to I: A pathway to interpersonal connectedness. *Journal of Personality and Social Psychology, 90,* 243-57.

p. 31   "A fundamentalist Christian and an atheist": Ibid., p. 245.

p. 32   "I was walking across a bridge": Phillips, E. (1999, June).
         The 75 funniest jokes of all time. *GQ*. Retrieved from http://
         www.emophilips.com/images/image-files/75-jokes.pdf.

p. 33   "People are comfortable with different worship styles": Em-
         erson & Smith, *Divided by faith*, p. 135.

p. 34   Toward fellow group members: Shariff, A. F. (2009, October).
         Religious prosociality: How Gods make us good. Paper pre-
         sented at the Society for the Scientific Study of Religion,
         Denver; Norenzayan, A., & Shariff, A. Z. (2008). The origin
         and evolution of religious prosociality. *Science*, 322, 58-62;
         Pichon, I., Boccato, G., Saroglou, V. (2007). Nonconscious
         influences of religion on prosociality: A priming study. *Eu-
         ropean Journal of Social Psychology*, 37, 1032-45; Preston, J.
         L., & Ritter, R. S. (2009). God or religion? Divergent effects
         on ingroup and outgroup altruism. Unpublished manuscript.
         As cited in Johnson, M., Rowatt, W., & LaBouff, J. (2010).
         Priming Christian religious concepts increases racial prej-
         udice. *Social Psychological and Personality Science*, 1, 119-26;
         Shariff, A. Z., & Norenzayan, A. (2007). God is watching
         you: Priming God concepts increases prosocial behavior in
         an anonymous economics game. *Psychological Science*, 18,
         803-9; Randolph-Seng, B., & Nielsen, M. E. (2007). Honesty:
         One effect of primed religious representation. *International
         Journal for the Psychology of Religion*, 17, 303-15; Carpenter,
         T. P., & Marshall, M. A. (2009). An examination of religious
         priming and intrinsic religious motivation in the moral hy-
         pocrisy paradigm. *Journal for the Scientific Study of Religion*,
         48, 386-93.

p. 34   Aggression toward nonmembers: Bushman, B. J., Ridge, R.
         D., Das, E., Key, C. W., & Busath, G. L. (2007). When God
         sanctions killing: Effect of scriptural violence on aggression.
         Psychological Science, 18, 204-7.

p. 34   Exact revenge on nonmembers: Saroglou, V., Corneille, O., &
         Van Cappellen, P. (2009). "Speak, Lord, your servant is lis-
         tening": Religious priming activates submissive thoughts

and behaviors. *International Journal for the Psychology of Religion, 19,* 143-54.

p. 34   Violence toward nonmembers: Ginges, J., Hansen, I., & Norenzayan, A. (2009). Religion and support for suicide attacks. *Psychological Science, 20,* 224-30.

pp. 35-36   "When God sets out to embrace the enemy": Volf, M. (1996). *Exclusion and embrace: A theological exploration of identity, otherness, and reconciliation.* Nashville: Abingdon, p. 129.

p. 36   "Because of Christ's blood": Felder, C. H. (1989). *Troubling biblical waters: Race, class and family.* Maryknoll, NY: Orbis Books, p. 157.

p. 37   "In the household of faith": DeYoung, C. (2009). *Coming together in the 21st century: The Bible's message in an age of diversity.* Valley Forge, VA: Judson Press, pp. 155-56.

p. 38   Kingdom of God is powerfully communicated to the world: McKnight, *A community called atonement*; see also Romans 16:17; 1 Corinthians 1:10-17; Ephesians 4:1-7, 12-13; 1 Peter 5:5; Acts 4:32; Hebrews 2:10-11.

p. 39   Diverse groups come up with more creative: O'Reilly, C. A., III, Caldwell, D. F., & Barnett, W. P. (1989). Work group demography, social integration and turnover. *Administrative Science Quarterly, 34,* 21-37.

p. 39   And more effective ideas: Cady, S., & Valentine, J. (1999). Team innovations and perceptions of consideration: What difference does diversity make? *Small Group Research, 30,* 730-50; McLeod, P. L., Lobel, S. A., & Cox, T. H., Jr. (1996). Ethnic diversity and creativity in small groups. *Small Group Research, 27,* 248-64.

p. 39   Bantel and Jackson assessed the diversity: Bantel, K., & Jackson, S. (1989). Top management and innovations in banking: Does the composition of the top team make a difference? *Strategic Management Journal, 10,* 107-24.

p. 39   Less unique information to the table: Marsh, J. G., as cited in Surowiecki, J. (2004). *The wisdom of crowds.* New York: Anchor.

p. 40   Express their opinions less frequently: Stasser, G., Stewart, D. D., & Wittenbaum, G. M. (1995, May). Expert roles and information exchange during discussion: The importance of knowing who knows what. *Journal of Experimental Social Psychology, 31,* 244-65; Rashotte, L. S., & Smith-Lovin, L. (1997). Who benefits from being bold? The interactive effects of task cues and status characteristics on influence in mock jury groups. *Advances in Group Processes, 14,* 235-55.

p. 40   Legitimate differences in opinion: Janis, I. L. (1972). *Victims of groupthink.* Boston: Houghton Mifflin; Janis, I. L. (1982). *Groupthink: Psychological studies of policy decisions and fiascos* (2nd ed.). Boston: Houghton Mifflin.

p. 40   Japanese threat to Pearl Harbor: Tetlock, P. E., McGuire, C., Peterson, R., Feld, P., & Chang, S. (1992). Assessing political group dynamics: A test of the groupthink model. *Journal of Personality and Social Psychology, 63,* 402-23.

p. 40   Former Presbyterian minister Gerald Tritle: Tritle, G. (unknown date). Groupthink: A sinister snare for elders and congregations alike [Web log post]. Retrieved from http://chalcedon.edu/research/articles/groupthink-a-sinister-snare-for-elders-and-congregations-alike/

p. 41   "Narcissism of small [doctrinal] differences": Tritle, G. (2011, January 18). The land was broad, quiet and peaceful. Retrieved from http://chnetwork.org/2011/01/gerald-tritle-the-land-was-broad-quiet-and-peaceful/

p. 42   Increasingly diverse and interconnected: Raschke, *The next reformation.*

Chapter 3

p. 44   Cognitive miser: Taylor, S., & Fiske, S. (1984). *Social cognition.* New York: Random House.

p. 45   To test this idea: Mendes, W. B., Blascovich, J., Hunter, S., Lickel, B., & Jost, J. (2007). Threatened by the unexpected: Physiological responses during social interactions with expectancy-violating partners. *Journal of Personality and Social Psychology, 92*, 698-716.

p. 47   Naïve psychologists: Heider, F. (1958). *The psychology of interpersonal relations.* New York: Wiley.

p. 48   Research on minimal groups: Tajfel, H. (1970). Experiments in intergroup discrimination. *Scientific American, 223*, 96-102.

p. 50   Charles Perdue and colleagues: Perdue, C. W., Dovidio, J. F., Gurtman, M. B., & Tyler, R. B. (1990). "Us" and "them": Social categorization and the process of intergroup bias. *Journal of Personality and Social Psychology, 59*, 475-86.

p. 51   Outgroup homogeneity effect: Quattrone, G. A., & Jones, E. E. (1980). The perception of variability within ingroups and out-groups: Implications for the law of small numbers. *Journal of Personality and Social Psychology, 38*, 141-52; Rubin, M., & Badea, C. (2012). They're all the same! . . . but for several different reasons: A review of the multicausal nature of perceived group variability. *Current Directions in Psychological Science, 21*, 367-72.

p. 51   Stuff White People Like: Lander, C. (2008). *Stuff white people like: The definitive guide to the unique taste of millions.* New York: Random House.

p. 53   Social psychologists have found that: Hills, P., & Lewis, M. (2006). Reducing the own-race bias in face recognition by shifting attention. *The Quarterly Journal of Experimental Psychology, 59*, 996-1002; Meissner, C., Brigham, J., & Butz, D. (2005). Memory for own- and other-race faces: A dual-process approach. *Applied Cognitive Psychology, 19*, 545-67; Pezdek, K., Blandon-Gitlin, I., & Moore, C. (2003). Children's face recognition memory: More evidence for the cross-race effect. *Journal of Applied Psychology, 88*, 760-63; Wright, D., Boyd, C., & Tredoux, C. (2003). Interracial contact and the own-race bias for face recognition in South Africa and England. *Applied Cognitive Psychology, 17*, 365-73.

p. 53   Patricia Linville: Linville, P. (1982). The complexity–extremity effect and age-based stereotyping. *Journal of Personality and Social Psychology, 42*, 193-211.

p. 55   Perceptions of outgroup homogeneity often lead to prejudice: Snyder, M., & Swann, W. (1978). Behavioral confirmation in social interaction: From social perception to social reality. *Journal of Experimental Social Psychology, 14*, 148-62; Snyder, M., & Swann, W. (1978). Hypothesis-testing processes in social interaction. *Journal of Personality and Social Psychology, 36*, 1202-12.

p. 56   Our meta-perceptions are wrought with miscalculations: Yzerbyt, V., Judd, C., & Muller, D. (2009). How do they see us? The vicissitudes of metaperception in intergroup relations. In S. Demoulin, J. Leyens & J. Dovidio (Eds.), *Intergroup misunderstandings: Impact of divergent social realities.* New York: Psychology Press.

p. 56   For example, research has shown: Judd, C. M., James-Hawkins, L., Yzerbyt, V. Y., & Kashima, Y. (2005). Fundamental dimensions of social judgment: Understanding the relations between competence and warmth. *Journal of Personality and Social Psychology, 89*, 899-913.

p. 56   Even groups based on socioeconomic: Yzerbyt, et al., How do they see us?

p. 58   Cognitive psychologists Kathleen McDermott and Henry Roediger: Roediger, H. L., & McDermott, K. B. (1995). Creating false memories: Remembering words not presented in lists. *Journal of Experimental Psychology: Learning, Memory and Cognition, 24*, 803-14.

p. 58   My friend and mentor Stan Klein: Klein, S. (1986). Untitled and unpublished manuscript, Department of Psychology, University of California, Santa Barbara.

p. 61   Outside our conscious awareness: Bargh, J. A., & Williams, L. E. (2006). The automaticity of social life. *Current Directions in Psychological Science, 15*, 1-4.

p. 61   Implicit attitude test: Retrieved from https://implicit.harvard.edu/implicit/

p. 61   Associate black men with violence and white men with non-violence: Payne, B. K. (2001). Prejudice and perception: The role of automatic and controlled processes in misperceiving a weapon. *Journal of Personality Social Psychology, 81*, 181-92.

p. 62   In my group identity research: Cleveland, C., Finez, L., Blascovich, J., & Ginther, N. (2012). For better or for worse: Superior and inferior teammate performance and changes in cardiovascular reactivity. *European Journal of Work and Organizational Psychology, 21*, 681-717.

p. 63   Remember the study in which nonsense syllables: Perdue et al., "Us" and "them."

p. 64   Research shows that the mere use of the word *we*: Ibid.

Chapter 4

p. 67   I recently conducted an experiment on team motivation: Cleveland, C., Finez, L., Blascovich, J., & Ginther, N. (2012). For better or for worse: Superior and inferior teammate performance and changes in cardiovascular reactivity. *European Journal of Work and Organizational Psychology, 21*, 681-717.

p. 70   This natural inclination to obsess over: Quattrone, G. A. (1986). On the perception of a group's variability. In S. Worchel & W. G. Austin (Eds.), *Psychology of intergroup relations* (2nd ed., pp. 25-48). Chicago: Nelson-Hall.

p. 70   This is called *perspective divergence*: Fiske, S., Harris, L., Russell, A., & Shelton, J. N. (2009). Divergent social realities, depending on where you sit: Perspectives from the stereotype content model. In S. Demoulin, J. Leyens & J. Dividio (Eds.), *Intergroup misunderstandings: Impact of divergent social realities* (pp. 173-90). New York: Psychology Press; Kessler, T., & Mummendey, A. (2009). Why do they not perceive us as we are? Ingroup projection as a source of intergroup misunderstanding. In S. Demoulin, J. Leyens & J. Dividio (Eds.), *Intergroup misunderstandings: Impact of divergent social realities* (pp. 135-52). New York: Psychology Press.

p. 71   Thomas Kessler, Amélie Mummendey and their colleagues: Kessler & Mummendey, Why do they not perceive us as we are?

p. 71   These researchers found that high school teachers: Ibid.

p. 73   In one study, Dominic Abrams: Abrams, D., Wetherell, M., Cochrane, S., Hogg, M., & Turner, J. (2001). Knowing what to think by knowing who you are: Self-categorization and the nature of norm formation, conformity and group polarization. In M. Hogg & D. Abrams (Eds.), *Intergroup relations* (pp. 270-88). New York: Psychology Press.

p. 74   "[Participants] resisted information": Ibid., p. 276.

p. 75   Groups that are aware of their similarities: Brewer, M. B. (1991). The social self: On being the same and different at the same time. *Personality and Social Psychology Bulletin, 17,* 475-82; Tajfel, H., & Turner, J. C. (1979). An integrative theory of intergroup conflict. In W. G. Austin & S. Worchel (Eds.), *The social psychology of intergroup relations* (pp. 33-47). Monterey, CA: Brooks/Cole; Tajfel, H., & Turner, J. C. (1986). The social identity theory of intergroup behavior. In S. Worchel & W. G. Austin (Eds.), *Psychology of intergroup relations* (pp. 7-24). Chicago: Nelson-Hall.

p. 75   Social identity researcher Richard Crisp: Crisp, R., & Beck, S. (2005). Reducing intergroup bias: The moderating role of ingroup identification. *Group Processes and Intergroup Relations, 8,* 173-85.

p. 77   According to prejudice researcher James Weyant: Weyant, J. (2007). Perspective taking as a means of reducing negative stereotyping of individuals who speak English as a second language. *Journal of Applied Social Psychology, 37,* 703-16.

p. 77   One study asked white students: Vescio, T. K., Sechrist, G. B., & Paolucci, M. P. (2003). Perspective taking and prejudice reduction: The mediational role of empathy arousal and situational attributions. *European Journal of Social Psychology, 33,* 455-72.

p. 77   "Looking at the world through his eyes": Galinsky, A. D., & Moskowitz, G. B. (2000). Perspective-taking: Decreasing stereotype expression, stereotype accessibility and ingroup favoritism. *Journal of Personality and Social Psychology, 78,* 708-24.

p. 77   Other studies have shown that perspective taking: Galinsky, A. D., & Ku, G. (2004). The effects of perspective-taking on prejudice: The moderating role of self-evaluation. *Personality and Social Psychology Bulletin, 30,* 594-604; Batson, C. D., Polycarpou, M. P., Harmon-Jones, E., Imhoff, H. J., Mitchener, E. C., Bednar, L. L., et al. (1997). Empathy and attitudes: Can feeling for a member of a stigmatized group improve feelings toward that group? *Journal of Personality and Social Psychology, 72,* 105-18; Weyant, Perspective taking as a means of reducing negative stereotyping.

Chapter 5

p. 81   Noted developmental psychologist Erik Erikson: Erickson, E. (1968). *Identity, youth and crisis.* New York: W. W. Norton Company.

p. 82   "Nothing dies harder than the desire": Eliot, T. S. (1932). Shakespeare and the stoicism of Seneca. *Selected Essays of T. S. Eliot.* New York: Faber and Faber.

p. 82   Early and important motivation theorist: Maslow, A. H. (1943). A theory of human motivation. *Psychological Review,* 50 (4), 370-96. Retrieved from http://psychclassics.yorku.ca/ Maslow/motivation.htm; Maslow, A. (1954). *Motivation and personality.* New York: Harper.

p. 82   First, according to *sociometer theory*: Leary, M. R., & Baumeister, R. F. (2000). The nature and function of self-esteem: Sociometer theory. In M. P. Zanna (Ed.), *Advances in experimental social psychology* (Vol. 32, pp. 1-62). San Diego: Academic Press; Leary, M. R., Tambor, E. S., Terdal, S. K., & Downs, D. L. (1995). Self-esteem as an interpersonal monitor: The sociometer hypothesis. *Journal of Personality and Social Psychology, 68,* 518-30.

p. 82   Second, *terror management theory*: Harmon-Jones, E., Simon, L., Greenberg, J., Pyszczynski, T., Solomon, S., & McGregor, H. (1997). Terror management theory and self-esteem: Evidence that increased self-esteem reduces mortality salience effects. *Journal of Personality and Social Psychology, 72,* 24-36.

p. 82   Third, high self-esteem: Crocker, J., & Wolfe, C. T. (2001). Contingencies of self-worth. *Psychological Review, 108,* 593-

623; Cutrona, C. E. (1982). Transition to college: Loneliness and the process of social adjustment. In L. A. Peplau & D. Perlman (Eds.), *Loneliness: A sourcebook of current theory, research, and therapy* (pp. 291-309). New York: Wiley; Brockner, J. (1979). The effects of self-esteem, success-failure and self-consciousness on task performance. *Journal of Personality and Social Psychology*, 37, 1732-41; Donnellan, M., Trzesniewski, K., Robins, R., Moffitt, T., & Caspi, A. (2005). Low self-esteem is related to aggression, anti-social behavior and delinquency. *Psychological Science, 16*, 328-35.

p. 83   We rely on feedback from other people: Cooley, C. (1902). *Human nature and the social order.* New York: Charles Scribner's Sons; Kenny, D., & DePaulo, B. (1993). Do people know how others view them? An empirical and theoretical account. *Psychological Bulletin, 114*, 145-61; Tice, D., & Wallace, H. (2005). The reflected self: Creating yourself as (you think) others see you. In M. R. Leary & J. P. Tangey (Eds.), *Handbook of self and identity* (pp. 91-105). New York: Guilford Press.

p. 83   "Your evaluation of your soul": Eldredge, J., & Curtis, B. (2001). The sacred romance: Drawing closer to the heart of God. Nashville: Thomas Nelson, p. 93.

p. 84   According to social identity theory: Tajfel, H., & Turner, J. C. (1979). An integrative theory of intergroup conflict. In W. G. Austin & S. Worchel (Eds.), *The social psychology of intergroup relations* (pp. 33-47). Monterey, CA: Brooks/Cole; Tajfel, H., & Turner, J. C. (1986). The social identity theory of intergroup behavior. In S. Worchel & W. G. Austin (Eds.), *Psychology of intergroup relations* (pp. 7-24). Chicago: Nelson-Hall.

p. 86   With respect to self-esteem: Ibid.

p. 86   We tend to stick with people who like what we like: Abrams, D., & Hogg, M. (2001). Collective identity, group membership and self-conception. In R. S. Tindale & M. Hogg (Eds.), *Blackwell handbook of social psychology: Group processes* (pp. 425-60). Oxford, UK: Blackwell.

p. 86   John Stott intuitively stated that: Stott, J. (1996). *The message of Ephesians.* Downers Grove, IL: IVP Academic, p. 148.

p. 86   A more cognitive explanation: Heider, F. (1946). Attitudes and cognitive organization. *The Journal of Psychology, 21,* 107-12; Heider, F. (1958). *The Psychology of interpersonal relations.* New York: John Wiley & Sons.

p. 88   "Bask in reflected glory": Cialdini, R., & DeNicholas, M. (1989). Self-presentation by association. *Personality and Social Psychology Bulletin, 57,* 626-31.

p. 88   In another study, Cialdini: Cialdini, R. B., Borden, R. J., Thorne, A., Walker, M. R., Freeman, S., & Sloan, L. R. (1976). Basking in reflected glory: Three (football) field studies. *Journal of Personality and Social Psychology, 34,* 366-75.

p. 89   "Cutting off reflected failure": Snyder, C. R., Lassegard, M., & Ford, C. E. (1986). Distancing after group success and failure: Basking in reflected glory and cutting off reflected failure. *Journal of Personality and Social Psychology, 51,* 382-88.

p. 89   In one important study, Snyder: Ibid.

p. 90   Some of my own research: Cleveland, C., Finez, L., Blascovich, J., & Ginther, N. (2012). For better or for worse: Superior and inferior teammate performance and changes in cardiovascular reactivity. *European Journal of Work and Organizational Psychology, 21,* 681-717.

p. 96   I recently watched a movie called *Music Within*: Donowho, B. (Producer), & Sawalich, S. (Director). (2007). *Music within* [Motion picture]. USA: The Weinstein Company.

p. 98   Research has shown that our awareness: Smith, E. R., Coats, S., & Watling, D. (1999). Overlapping mental representations of self, ingroup and partner: Further response-time evidence and a connectionist model. *Personality and Social Psychology Bulletin, 25,* 873-82.

p. 99   When a certain identity is in the forefront: Ibid.

p. 99   Researchers who study close relationships: Aron, A., Aron, E. N., Tudor, M., & Nelson, G. (1991). Close relationships as including other in the self. *Journal of Personality and Social Psychology, 60,* 241-53; Aron, A., Aron, E. N., & Norman, C.

(2001). The self expansion model of motivation and cognition in close relationships and beyond. In M. Clark & G. Fletcher (Eds.), *Blackwell handbook in social psychology: Vol. 2. Interpersonal processes* (pp. 478-501). Oxford: Blackwell.

p. 100   Noted groups researcher John Turner: Turner, J. (1982). Towards a cognitive redefinition of the social group. In H. Tajfel (Ed.), *Social identity and intergroup relations* (pp. 15-40). Cambridge, UK: Cambridge University Press.

Chapter 6

p. 102   Back in 1951: Hastorf, A. H., & Cantril, H. (1954). They saw a game: A case study. *Journal of Abnormal and Social Psychology, 49,* 129-34.

p. 102   Not only do we use our group: Leary, M. R. (2007). Motivational and emotional aspects of the self. *Annual Review of Psychology, 58,* 317-44.

p. 103   One way we engage in self-serving biases: Erber, R., & Tesser, A. (1994). Self-evaluation maintenance: A social psychological approach to interpersonal relationships. In I. R. Erber & R. Gilmour (Eds.), *Theoretical frameworks for personal relationships* (pp. 211-33). Hillsdale, NJ: Erlbaum.

p. 103   Second is to make self-serving attributions: Brown, J. D., & Rogers, R. J. (1991). Self-serving attributions: The role of physiological arousal. *Personality and Social Psychology Bulletin, 17,* 501-6.

p. 103   A third way we employ self-serving biases: Tesser, A. (1988). Toward a self-evaluation maintenance model of social behavior. In L. Berkowitz (Ed.), *Advances in experimental social psychology* (Vol. 21, pp. 181-227). San Diego: Academic Press.

p. 103   Well, North Americans tend to feel pretty good: Twenge, J. M., & Campbell, W. K. (2001). Age and birth cohort differences in self-esteem: A cross-temporal analysis. *Personality and Social Psychology Review, 5,* 321-44; Kitayama, S., Markus, H. R., Matsumoto, H., & Norasakkunkit, V. (1997). Individual and collective processes in the construction of the self: Self-enhancement in the United States and self-depreciation in Japan. *Journal of Personality and Social Psychology, 72,* 1245-67.

p. 103   Almost everyone rates themselves as better than average: Alicke, M. D., & Govorun, O. (2005). The better-than-average effect. In M. D. Alicke, D. A. Dunning & J. I. Kruger (Eds.), *The self in social judgment* (pp. 85-106). New York: Psychology Press.

p. 104   Since our self-esteem is so closely tied to group membership: Abrams, D., & Hogg, M. (2001). Comments on the motivational status of self-esteem in social identity and intergroup discrimination. In M. Hogg & D. Abrams (Eds.), *Intergroup Relations* (pp. 232-44). New York: Psychology Press.

p. 105   The unfortunate truth: Fein, S., & Spencer, S. (1997). Prejudice as a self-esteem maintenance: Affirming the self through derogating others. *Journal of Personality and Social Psychology, 73,* 31-44.

p. 105   Two social psychologists, Steven Fein and Steven Spencer: Ibid.

p. 107   Research conducted by Fein and Spencer and others: Ibid.; Abrams & Hogg, Comments on the motivational status of self-esteem.

p. 111   One possible sign that you have succumbed: Abrams, D., Wetherell, M., Cochrane, S., Hogg, M., & Turner, J. (2001). Knowing what to think by knowing who you are: Self-categorization and the nature of norm formation, conformity and group polarization. In M. Hogg & D. Abrams (Eds.), *Intergroup relations* (pp. 270-88). New York: Psychology Press.

p. 112   I believe that self-affirmation theory can help: Steele, C. M. (1988). The psychology of self-affirmation: Sustaining the integrity of the self. In L. Berkowitz (Ed.), *Advances in experimental social psychology* (Vol. 21). Orlando: Academic Press.

p. 112   When people affirm another aspect of their self: Ibid.; Sherman, D., & Cohen, G. (2006). The psychology of self-defense: Self-affirmation theory. In M. P. Zanna (Ed.), *Advances in experimental social psychology* (Vol. 38, pp. 183-242). San Diego: Academic Press; Sherman, D. K., & Cohen, G. L. (2002). Accepting threatening information: Self-affirmation and the reduction of defensive biases. *Current Directions in Psychological Science, 11*, 119-23.

p. 115   My friends David Sherman and Heejung Kim: Sherman, D. K., & Kim, H. S. (2005). Is there an "I" in "team"? The role of the self in group-serving judgments. *Journal of Personality and Social Psychology, 88*, 108-20.

p. 115   They also found that self-affirmation: Sherman, D., Kinias, Z., Major, B., Kim, H., & Prenovost, M. (2007). The group as a resource: Reducing biased attributions for group success and failure via self-affirmation. *Personality and Social Psychology Bulletin, 33*, 1100-1112.

p. 115   And most recently, they've found that: Cohen, G., Sherman, D., Bastardi, A., Hsu, L., McGoey, M., & Ross, L. (2007). Bridging the partisan divide: Self-affirmation reduces ideological closed-mindedness and inflexibility in negotiation. *Journal of Personality and Social Psychology, 93*, 415-30.

Chapter 7

p. 118   We tend to have a difficult time seeing: Abrams, D., Wetherell, M., Cochrane, S., Hogg, M., & Turner, J. (2001). Knowing what to think by knowing who you are: Self-categorization and the nature of norm formation, conformity and group polarization. In M. Hogg & D. Abrams (Eds.), *Intergroup relations* (pp. 270-88). New York: Psychology Press.

p. 120   In one episode: Ehrin, K. (Writer), & Liddi-Brown, A. (Director). (2006). Who's your daddy? [Television series episode]. In P. Berg (Executive Producer), *Friday Night Lights*. Los Angeles: NBC Universal Television.

p. 121   Muzafer Sherif's classic research: Sherif, M., Harvey, O. J., White, B. J., & Sherif, C. (1961). *Intergroup conflict and cooperation: The robbers cave experiment*. Norman: University of Oklahoma Institute of Group Relations.

p. 121   Finally, in the 1970s: Zechmeister, J., Zechmeister, E., & Shaughnessy, J. (2001). *Essentials of research methods in psychology*. Boston: McGraw-Hill.

p. 122   "You can tell those guys": Baumeister, R., & Bushman, B.
           (2008). *Social psychology and human nature*. Belmont, CA:
           Thomson, p. 413.

p. 123   By the end, Sherif noted: Sherif et al., *Intergroup conflict and
           cooperation*, p. 85.

p. 123   Realistic conflict theory: Levine, R. A., & Campbell, D. T.
           (1972). *Ethnocentrism: Theories of conflict, ethnic attitudes
           and group behavior*. New York: Wiley.

p. 124   The lynching of African Americans: Tolnay, S., & Beck, E. M.
           (1995). *A festival of violence: An analysis of southern lynchings,
           1982-1930*. Champaign: University of Illinois Press.

p. 124   People are less tolerant of immigrants: O'Rourke, K. H., &
           Sinnott, R. (2006). The determinants of individual attitudes
           towards immigration. *European Journal of Political Economy*,
           22, 838-61.

p. 126   Michael Zarate and colleagues: Zarate, M., Garcia, B., Garza,
           A., & Hitlan, R. (2004). Cultural threat and perceived real-
           istic group conflict as dual predictors of prejudice. *Journal of
           Experimental Social Psychology*, 40, 99-105.

p. 127   Whether we are trained in psychology or not: Heider, F.
           (1958). *The psychology of interpersonal relations*. New York:
           Wiley.

p. 127   Individual's "need for a firm answer": Kruglanski, A. (2004).
           The psychology of closed mindedness. New York: Psychology
           Press, p. 6.

p. 127   For example, theologian Scot McKnight: McKnight, S.
           (2007). *A community called atonement*. Nashville: Abingdon.

p. 128   Kruglanski and colleagues have found: Kruglanski, A. W.,
           Webster, D. M., & Klem, A. (1993). Motivated resistance and
           openness to persuasion in the presence or absence of prior
           information. *Journal of Personality and Social Psychology*, 65,
           861-76.

p. 128   According to Kruglanski: Kruglanski, A. W., & Webster, D.
           M. (1996). Motivated closing of the mind: Seizing and
           freezing. *Psychological Review*, 103, 263-83.

p. 129   Black sheep effect: Marques, J., Yzerbyt, V., & Leyens, J. (1988). The "black sheep effect": Extremity of judgments towards ingroup members as a function of group identification. *European Journal of Social Psychology, 18*, 1-16.

p. 130   Recently, my colleagues and I: Frings, D., Hurst, J., Cleveland, C., Blascovich, J., & Abrams, D. (2012). Challenge, threat and subjective group dynamics: Reactions to normative and deviant group members. *Group Dynamics: Theory, Research & Practice, 16*, 105-21.

p. 132   "What does truth have to fear?": Boyd, G. (2011, March 4). Rob Bell is NOT a universalist (and I actually read "Love Wins"). [Web log post]. Retrieved from http://reknew.org /2011/03/rob-bell-is-not-a-universalist-and-i-actually-read-love-wins/

p. 132   E. Tory Higgins: Higgins, E. T. (1997). Beyond pleasure and pain. *American Psychologist, 52*, 1280-1300.

p. 133   Both promotion and prevention orientations: Crowe, E., & Higgins, E. T. (1997). Regulatory focus and strategic inclinations: Promotion and prevention in decision making. *Organizational Behavior and Human Decision Processes, 69*, 117-32.

p. 134   "Negative information weighs more heavily": Ito, T. A., Larsen, J. T., Smith, N. K., & Cacioppo, J. T. (1998). Negative information weighs more heavily on the brain: The negativity bias in evaluative categorizations. *Journal of Personality and Social Psychology, 75*, 887.

p. 136   "When You and I are 'We'": Gardner, W. L., Gabriel, S., & Hochschild, L. (2002). When you and I are "we," you are not threatening: The role of self-expansion in social comparison. *Journal of Personality and Social Psychology, 82*, 239-51.

p. 136   Matthew Hornsey and colleagues: Hornsey, M. J., & Imani, A. (2004). Criticizing groups from the inside and the outside: An identity perspective on the intergroup sensitivity effect. *Personality and Social Psychology Bulletin, 30*, 365-83.

Chapter 8

p. 140   Religion and culture are easily confused: Cohen, A. (2009).
            Many forms of culture. *American Psychologist, 64*, 94-104.

p. 140   Psychology textbook authors: Kassin, S., Fein, S., & Markus,
            H. R. (2008). *Social psychology* (7th ed.). New York:
            Houghton Mifflin.

p. 140   Compare that with sociologist Emile Durkheim's: Durkheim, E.
            (1995). *Elementary forms of religious life* (K. E. Fields, Trans.).
            New York: Free Press, p. 44. (Original work published 1912).

p. 140   Anthropologist Clifford Geertz: Geertz, C. (1973). *Interpre-
            tation of cultures: Selected essays by Clifford Geertz*. New York:
            Basic Books, p. 90.

p. 140   Cultural psychologist Joni Sasaki and I: Cleveland, C., &
            Sasaki, J. (2011). Amazing grace: Cultural differences in
            Protestant theology and self-awareness. Presented at the
            Annual Meeting of the Society for Personality and Social Psy-
            chology, San Antonio.

p. 141   The good news is that research: Kimmel, A. (1996). *Ethical
            issues in behavioral research: A survey*. Cambridge, MA:
            Blackwell.

p. 141   The use of deception remains: Zechmeister, J., Zechmeister,
            E., & Shaughnessy, J. (2001). *Essentials of research methods in
            psychology*. Boston: McGraw-Hill.

p. 141   For good reason, researchers (such as myself): Kelman, H.
            (1972). The rights of the subject in social research: An
            analysis of relative power and legitimacy. *American Psychol-
            ogist, 27*, 989-1016.

p. 143   The confusion caused by the similarity of religion and
            culture: Cohen, Many forms of culture.

p. 143   Philosopher Charles Taylor: Taylor, C. (1989). *Sources of the
            self: The making of the modern identity*. Cambridge, MA:
            Harvard University Press.

p. 144   Church growth and evangelism professor Soong-chan Rah:
            Rah, S.-C. (2009). *The next evangelicalism: Freeing the church*

from western cultural captivity. Downers Grove, IL: Inter-Varsity Press.

p. 144   Cultural psychologist Adam Cohen: Cohen, A. B., Hall, D. E., Koenig, H. G., & Meador, K. G. (2005). Social versus individual motivation: Implications for normative definitions of religious orientation. *Personality & Social Psychology Review*, *9*, 48-61.

p. 145   Cultural psychologists have studied: Markus, H. R., & Kitayama, S. (1991). Culture and the self: Implications for cognition, emotion and motivation. *Psychological Review*, *98*, 224-53.

p. 146   For example, studies show that individualistic Americans: Cohen et al., Social versus individual motivation.

p. 147   Research suggests that diversity initiatives: Engleberg, I., & Wynn, D. (2007). *Working in groups.* New York: Houghton Mifflin.

p. 149   Biblical scholar Robert Tannehill: Tannehill, R. C. (1994). *The narrative unity of Luke-Acts: A literary interpretation.* Minneapolis: Fortress, p. 185.

p. 149   Interestingly, invoking common group membership: Sherif, M., Harvey, O. J., White, B. J., & Sherif, C. (1961). *Intergroup conflict and cooperation: The robbers cave experiment.* Norman: University of Oklahoma Institute of Group Relations.

p. 149   In fact, much research suggests: Gaertner, S., Mann, J., Murrell, A., & Dovidio, J. (2001). Reducing intergroup bias: The benefits of recategorization. In M. Hogg & D. Abrams (Eds.), *Intergroup relations* (pp. 356-69). New York: Psychology Press.

Chapter 9

p. 153   Gordon Allport, an early groups theorist: Kassin, S., Fein, S., & Markus, H. R. (2008). *Social psychology* (7th ed.). New York: Houghton Mifflin, p. 172.

p. 153   Allport recognized that homogeneity is never harmless: Allport, G. (1954). *The nature of prejudice.* Cambridge, MA: Addison-Wesley.

p. 154   Crosscultural contact has often been described as an exercise in error reduction: Tausch, N., Kenworthy, J., & Hewstone, M. (2006). Intergroup contact and the improvement of intergroup relations. In M. Fitzduff & C. Stout (Eds.), *The psychology of resolving global conflicts: From war to peace* (Vol. 2, pp. 67-107). Westport, CT: Praeger Security International.

p. 154   As a bonus, contact reduces the anxiety: Wright, S. (2009). Cross-group contact effects. In S. Otten, K. Sassenberg & T. Kessler (Eds.), *Intergroup relations: The role of motivation and emotion* (pp. 262-83). New York: Psychology Press.

p. 154   Crosscultural contact based on contact theory has worked wonders: Tausch et al., Intergroup contact.

p. 154   Hundreds of studies have shown: Pettigrew, T., & Tropp, L. (2006). A meta-analytic test of intergroup contact theory. *Journal of Personality and Social Psychology, 90,* 751-83.

p. 154   Teachers who had previously interacted with an HIV-positive individual: Greenland, K., Masser, B., & Prentice, T. (2001). "They're scared of it": Intergroup determinants of attitudes toward children with HIV. *Journal of Applied Social Psychology, 31,* 2127-48.

p. 154   Crosscultural contact works its magic by: Tausch et al., Intergroup contact.

p. 155   Recent research has demonstrated that crosscultural contact: Pettigrew & Tropp, A meta-analytic test; Tausch et al., Intergroup contact; Smith, E. (1993). Social identity and social emotions: Toward new conceptualizations of prejudice. In D. M. Mackie & D. L. Hamilton (Eds.), *Affect, cognition, and stereotyping* (pp. 297-315). San Diego: Academic Press; Doosje, B., Branscombe, N., Spears, R., & Manstead, A. (1998). Guilty by association: When one's group has a negative history. *Journal of Personality and Social Psychology, 75,* 872-86; Stephan, W., & Finlay, K. (1999). The role of empathy in improving intergroup relations. *Journal of Social Issues, 55,* 729-43.

p. 155   Simple contact between groups does not necessarily improve attitudes: Dixon, J., & Reicher, S. (1997). Intergroup contact and desegregation in the new South Africa. *British*

Journal of Social Psychology, 36, 361-81; Forbes, H. (1997). *Ethnic conflict: Commerce, culture, and the contact hypothesis.* New Haven, CT: Yale University Press; Taylor, M. (1998). How white attitudes vary with the racial composition of local populations: Numbers count. *American Sociological Review, 63*, 512-35.

p. 155   Gordon Allport once wrote: Allport, *The nature of prejudice.*

p. 157   As sociologists Michael Emerson and Christian Smith: Emerson, M., & Smith, C. (2000). *Divided by faith: Evangelical religion and the problem of race in America.* New York: Oxford University Press.

p. 158   Muzafer Sherif, the lead researcher on the study: Sherif, M., Harvey, O. J., White, B. J., & Sherif, C. (1961). *Intergroup conflict and cooperation: The robbers cave experiment.* Norman: University of Oklahoma Institute of Group Relations.

p. 159   For example, Greeks and Turks: Kinzer, G. (1999, September 13). Earthquakes help warm Greek-Turk relations. *The New York Times.* Retrieved from http://www.nytimes.com/1999/09/13/world/earthquakes-help-warm-greek-turkish-relations.html?pagewanted=all&src=pm

p. 159   Jigsaw classroom approach: Aronson, E., Blaney, N., Stephin, C., Sikes, J., & Snapp, M. (1978). *The jigsaw classroom.* Beverly Hills: Sage.

p. 161   Earlier I mentioned Scot McKnight's book: McKnight, S. (2007). *A community called atonement.* Nashville: Abingdon.

p. 166   Miroslav Volf argues that both reconciliation and justice: Volf, M. (1996). *Exclusion and embrace: A theological exploration of identity, otherness, and reconciliation.* Nashville: Abingdon.

p. 167   Peggy McIntosh's "The Invisible Knapsack": McIntosh, P. (1988). White privilege and pale privilege: A personal account of coming to see correspondences through work in Women's Studies. Wellesley, MA: Wellesley College Center for Research on Women.

p. 167   Ifat Moaz found that in structured, crosscultural encounters: Moaz, I. (2000). An experiment in peace: Reconciliation-aimed workshops of Jewish-Israeli and Palestinian Youth. *Journal of Peace Research, 37,* 721-36.

p. 168   What Volf calls "psychological homelessness": Volf, *Exclusion and embrace,* p. 184.

p. 168   American Christians (who tend to be highly individualistic): Cohen, A. B., Hall, D. E., Koenig, H. G., & Meador, K. G. (2005). Social versus individual motivation: Implications for normative definitions of religious orientation. *Personality & Social Psychology Review, 9,* 48-61.

p. 168   Nancy Schlossburg introduced the concepts of mattering and marginality: Schlossburg, N. (1989). Mattering and marginality: Key issues in building community. *New Directions for Student Services, 48,* 1-7.

p. 170   A good amount of research suggests that diversity: Stangor, C. (2004). *Social groups in action and interaction.* New York: Psychology Press.

p. 170   Crosscultural groups often perform worse than homogenous groups: Timmerman, T. (2000). Racial diversity, age diversity, interdependence and team performance. *Small Group Research, 31,* 592-606.

p. 170   Crosscultural group members tend to communicate with each other less: Hoffman, E. (1985). The effect of race-ration composition on the frequency of organizational communication. *Social Psychology Quarterly, 48,* 17-26.

p. 170   React to each other with more emotional negativity: Cunningham, G. B., & Sagas, M. (2004). Group diversity, occupational commitment, and occupational turnover intentions among NCAA Division IA football coaching staffs. *Journal of Sport Management, 18,* 236-54.

p. 170   They are less satisfied with the group: Mueller, C., Finley, A., Iverson, R., & Price, J. (1999). The effects of group racial composition on job satisfaction, organizational commitment and career commitment: The case of teachers. *Work and Occupations, 26,* 187-219.

p. 170   Experience less psychological closeness: Tsui, A. S., Egan, T.

D., & O'Reilly, C. A. (1992). Being different: Relational demography and organizational attachment. *Administrative Science Quarterly, 37,* 547-79.

p. 170 Perceive less supervisor support: Jeanquart-Barone, S. (1996). Implications of racial diversity in the supervisor-subordinate relationship. *Journal of Applied Social Psychology, 26,* 935-44.

p. 170 Experience less procedural justice: Ibid.

p. 171 When we get to know culturally different people: Cook, S. (1978). Interpersonal and attitudinal outcomes in cooperating interracial groups. *Journal of Research and Development in Education, 12,* 97-113.

p. 171 Research on crosscultural relationships between Catholics and Protestants: Leyens, J., Paladino, M., Rodriguez, R., Vaes, J., Demoulin, S., Rodriguez, A., & Gaunt, R. (2000). The emotional side of prejudice: The attribution of secondary emotions to ingroups and outgroups. *Personality and Social Psychology Review, 4,* 186-97.

p. 172 Perhaps the most important reason why personal interaction is so valuable: Tausch et al., Intergroup contact.

p. 173 When it comes to crosscultural unity, leadership is vital: Ibid.

p. 173 Long ago, Pettigrew argued: Pettigrew, T. (1971). *Racially separate or together?* New York: McGraw-Hill.

p. 173 The extended-contact hypothesis: Wright, S., Aron, A., McLaughlin-Volpe, T., & Ropp, S. (1997). The extended contact effect: Knowledge of cross-group friendships and prejudice. *Journal of Personality and Social Psychology, 73,* 73-90.

p. 174 Crosscultural contact in places like South Africa: Pettigrew, T. (1998). Intergroup contact theory. *Annual Review of Psychology, 49,* 65-85.

p. 174 And Northern Ireland: Hughes, J. (2001). Constitutional reform in Northern Ireland: Implications for community relations policy and practice. *The International Journal of Conflict Management, 12,* 257-82.

p. 175   Group members who hail from low-status groups: Rashotte,
              L., & Smith-Lovin, L. (1997). Who benefits from being bold:
              The interactions effects of task cues and status characteristics
              on influence in mock jury groups. *Advances in group pro-
              cesses* (Vol. 14). Stamford, CT: JAI Press; Stasser, G., Stewart,
              D., & Wittenbaum, G. (1995). Expert roles and information
              exchange during discussion: The importance of knowing
              who knows what. *Journal of Experimental Social Psychology*,
              31, 244-65.

p. 175   Group members who hail from higher-status groups: Wit-
              tenbaum, G. (1998). Information sampling in decision-
              making groups: The impact of members' task-relevant status.
              Small Group Research, *29*, 57-84.

p. 175   Since group leaders have high status in the group: Larson, J.,
              Christensen, C., Abbott, A., & Franz, T. (1996). Diagnosing
              groups: Charting the flow of information in medical de-
              cision-making teams. *Journal of Personality and Social Psy-
              chology*, *71*, 315-70.

Chapter 10

p. 178   Common ingroup identity model: Gaertner, S. L., Dovidio, J.
              F., Anastasio, P. A., Bachman, B. A., & Rust, M. C. (1993).
              The Common Ingroup Identity Model: Recategorization and
              the reduction of intergroup bias. *European Review of Social
              Psychology*, *4*, 1-26.

p. 178   "If members of different groups": Gaertner, S. L. , & Dovidio,
              J. F. (2005). Categorization, recategorization and intergroup
              bias. In J. F. Dovidio, P. Glick & L. Rudman. *Reflecting on the
              Nature of Prejudice*. Philadelphia: Psychology Press.

p. 179   In one study: Nier, J. A., Gaertner, S. L., Dovidio, J. F., Banker,
              B. S., & Ward, C. M. (2001). Changing interracial evalua-
              tions and behavior: The effects of a common group identity.
              Group Processes and Intergroup Relations, *4*, 299-316.

p. 179   Another study found that British college students: Stone, C.
              H., & Crisp, R. J. (2007). Superordinate and subgroup iden-
              tification as predictors of intergroup evaluation in common

ingroup contexts. *Group Processes and Intergroup Relations,* *10,* 493-513.

p. 179   Plus, when we know that *they:* Gómez, A., Dovidio, J. F., Huici, C., Gaertner, S. L., & Cuadrado, I. (2008). The other side of we: When outgroup members express common identity. *Personality and Social Psychology Bulletin, 34,* 1613-26.

p. 180   Wendi Gardner and colleagues suggest: Gardner, W. L., Gabriel, S., & Hochschild, L. (2002). When you and I are "we," you are not threatening: The role of self-expansion in social comparison. *Journal of Personality and Social Psychology, 82,* 239-51.

p. 181   Indeed, when we adopt a common identity: Hornsey, M. J., & Imani, A. (2004). Criticizing groups from the inside and the outside: An identity perspective on the intergroup sensitivity effect. *Personality and Social Psychology Bulletin, 30,* 365-83.

p. 182   Research shows that crosscultural situations that lack forgiveness: McCullough, M. E., Bellah, C. G., Kilpatrick, S. D., & Johnson, J. L. (2001). Vengefulness: Relationships with forgiveness, rumination, well-being and the big five. *Personality and Social Psychology Bulletin, 27,* 601-10; Tutu, D. (1999). *No future without forgiveness.* New York: Random House.

p. 182   Michael Wohl and Nyla Branscombe tested this idea with Jewish participants: Wohl, M. J. A., & Branscombe, N. R. (2005). Forgiveness and collective guilt assignment to historical perpetrator groups depend on level of social category inclusiveness. *Journal of Personality and Social Psychology, 88,* 288-303.

p. 183   The average Native Canadian's income: Russell, B. (1998). *Records of the federal Department of Indian Affairs at the National Archives of Canada: A source for genealogical research.* Toronto: Ontario Genealogical Society.

p. 183   Native Canadians suffer from society-wide discrimination: Lock Kunz, J., Milan, A., & Schetagne, S. (2000). *Unequal access: A Canadian profile of racial differences in education, employment and income.* Toronto: Canadian Race Relations Foundation.

p. 184   Diverse groups are more creative: O'Reilly, C. A., III, Caldwell,
          D. F., & Barnett, W. P. (1989). Work group demography,
          social integration and turnover. *Administrative Science Quar-
          terly, 34,* 21-37.

p. 184   Generate more feasible and effective ideas: Cady, S., & Val-
          entine, J. (1999). Team innovations and perceptions of con-
          sideration: What difference does diversity make? *Small
          Group Research, 30,* 730-50; McLeod, P. L., Lobel, S. A., &
          Cox, T. H., Jr. (1996). Ethnic diversity and creativity in small
          groups. *Small Group Research, 27,* 248-64.

p. 184   However, this is only the case if all group members feel heard:
          Timmerman, T. (2000). Racial diversity, age diversity, inter-
          dependence and team performance. *Small Group Research,
          31,* 592-606.

p. 185   A sports psychologist named George Cunningham: Cun-
          ningham, G. B., & Sagas, M. (2004). Group diversity, occu-
          pational commitment and occupational turnover intentions
          among NCAA Division IA football coaching staffs. *Journal of
          Sport Management, 18,* 236-54.

p. 185   In an experimental field study: Nier et al., Changing inter-
          racial evaluations and behavior.

p. 186   We like them more: Brewer, M. (1979). Ingroup bias in the
          minimal intergroup situation: A cognitive-motivational
          analysis. *Psychological Bulletin, 86,* 307-24; Messick, D., &
          Mackie, D. (1989). Intergroup relations. *Annual Review of
          Psychology, 40,* 45-81; Tajfel, H. (1969). Cognitive aspects of
          prejudice. *Journal of Social Issues, 25,* 79-97; Wilder, D. A.
          (1986). Social categorization: Implications for creation and
          reduction of intergroup bias. *Advances in experimental social
          psychology, 19,* 291-355.

p. 186   Believe that we share more beliefs and values: Wilder, D. A.
          (1984). Intergroup contact: The typical member and the ex-
          ception to the rule. *Journal of Experimental Social Psychology,
          20,* 177-94; Brown, R. J., & Abrams, D. (1986). The effects of
          intergroup similarity and goal interdependence on inter-
          group attitudes and task performance. *Journal of Experi-*

mental Social Psychology, 22, 21-33; Brown, R. J. (1984). The role of similarity in intergroup relations. In H. Tajfel (Ed.), *The social dimension* (Vol. 2, pp. 603-23). Cambridge: Cambridge University Press; Hogg, M. & Turner, J. (1985). When liking begets solidarity: An experiment on the role of interpersonal attraction in psychological group formation. *British Journal of Social Psychology, 24,* 267-81.

p. 186   Remember more positive things about them: Howard, J., & Rothbart, M. (1980). Social categorization and memory for ingroup and outgroup behavior. *Journal of Personality and Social Psychology, 38,* 301-10.

p. 186   Less inclined to blame them for accidents: Hewstone, M., Bond, M., & Wan, K. (1983). Social facts and social attributions: The explanation of intergroup differences in Hong Kong. *Social Cognition, 2,* 142-57; Wang, G., & McKillip, J. (1978). Ethnic identification and judgments of an accident. *Personality and Social Psychology Bulletin, 4,* 296-99.

p. 187   Volf partially defines exclusion: Volf, M. (1996). *Exclusion and embrace: A theological exploration of identity, otherness, and reconciliation.* Nashville: Abingdon.

p. 187   "The other then emerges as an inferior being": Ibid., p. 67.

p. 187   Gaertner and Dovidio are quick to point out: Gaertner, S., Mann, J., Murrell, A., & Dovidio, J. (2001). Reducing intergroup bias: The benefits of recategorization. In M. Hogg & D. Abrams (Eds.), *Intergroup relations* (pp. 356-69). New York: Psychology Press.

p. 187   Research on color-blind policies in integrated schools: Schofield, J. W. (2001). The colorblind perspective in school: Causes and consequences. In J. A. Banks & C. A. McGee Banks (Eds.), *Multicultural education: Issues & perspectives* (4th ed., pp. 247-67). New York: Wiley.

p. 188   To show that this is possible, Gaertner and colleagues: Gaertner, S. L., Dovidio, J. F., Rust, M. C., Nier, J., Banker, B., Ward, C. M., et al. (1999). Reducing intergroup bias: Elements of intergroup cooperation. *Journal of Personality and Social Psychology, 76,* 388-402.

p. 189   Indeed, racial bias researcher Jennifer Richeson: Richeson, J.
            A., & Nussbaum, R. J. (2004). The impact of multicultur-
            alism versus color-blindness on racial bias. *Journal of Experi-
            mental Social Psychology, 40,* 417-23.

p. 189   "Jesus creates a new family": Clapp, R. (1993). *Families at the
            crossroads: Beyond traditional and modern options.* Downers
            Grove, IL: InterVarsity Press, p. 77.

p. 190   "He [Jesus] corrupts the young people": Thiessen, G., as
            cited in ibid.